AF267225

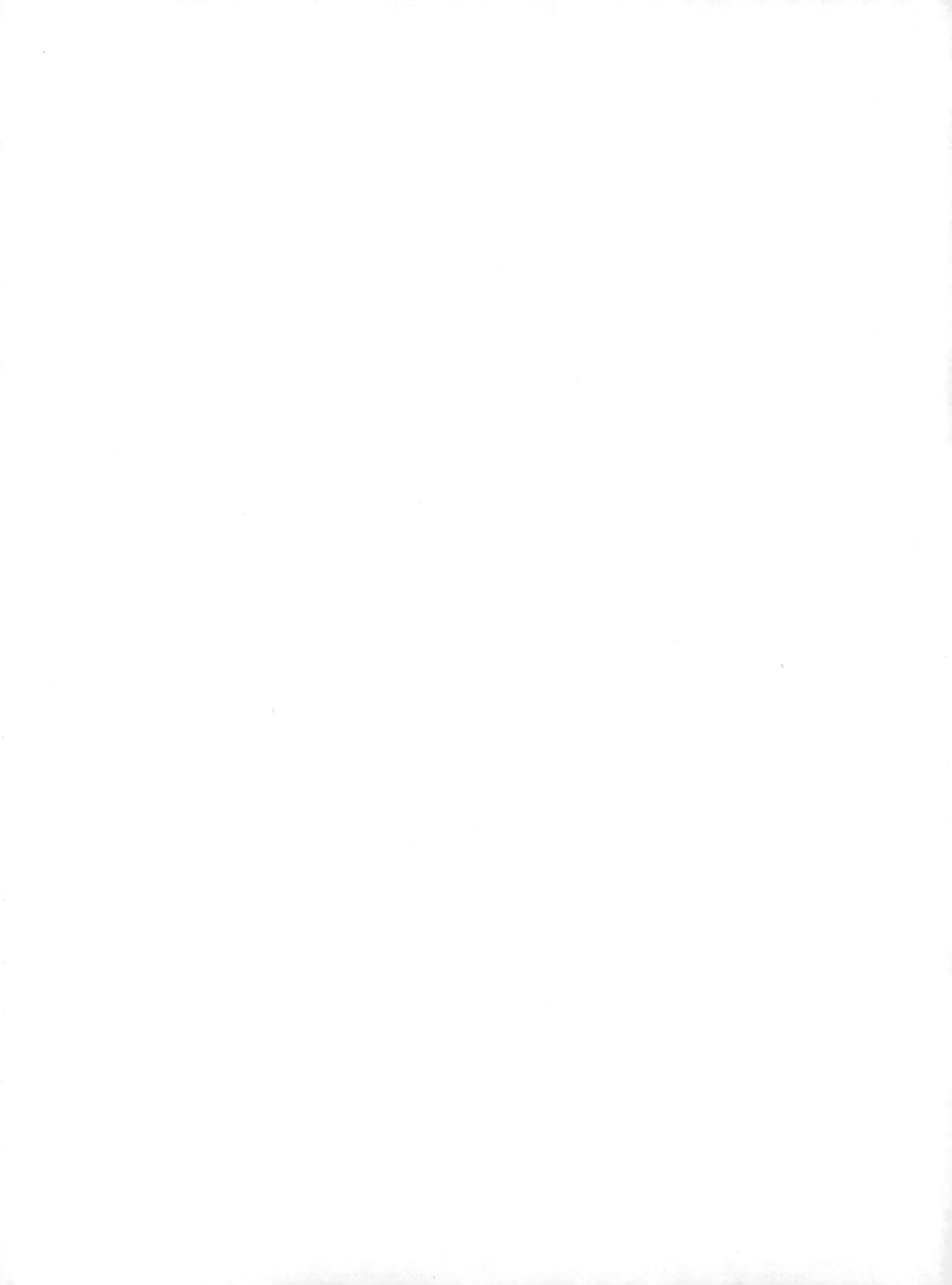

INCUNABULÆ

COLLECTED WORKS, 1990 – 2015

Kurt Slauson

ISBN: 978-0-9978256-7-1
Run Amok Books, 2017
First Edition

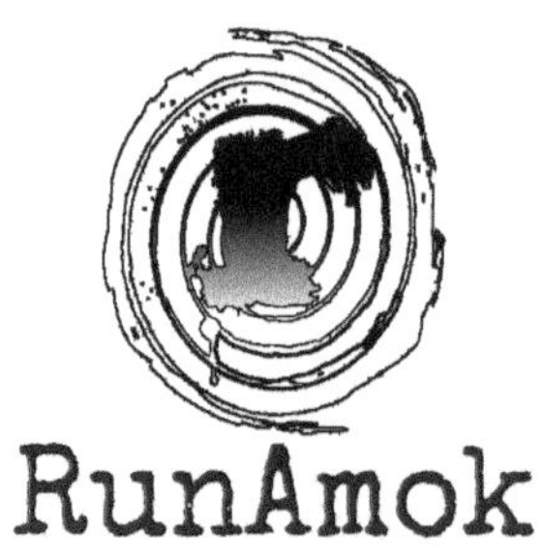

RunAmok

Printed in the U.S.A.

for Maya and Owen

CONTENTS

Acknowledgements   i
Foreword: by Ed Skoog   iii
I PAINTINGS   1
II DRAWINGS   35
III POEMS   65
Longing Looks At Longing   69
Each To Each   70
Carny   72
The Shite-Fighter's Destiny   74
Death Of A Sale   76
Marxist Zamboni Driver   77
Trumpet Vine   78
Christmas 2004   79
Divorce   80
In Theory   81
New Or Better   82
Shocking Door   83
Subtly Found Grand Legacy   84
All Springs   86
Sufficiently Underwhelmed   87
Addiction Deftly   88
Christmas 2006   89
Boy Meets Extinction   90
Poem   91
Anything For Love   92
Ascending Ape Setback   93
Curiousest Of Curios   94
Farm In Fall   95
Feminist Destiny Haiku Test Site   96
Healing For Birds   97
Incongruous Eagle Scout   98
Supine Boxing Theorem   99
For The Birds   100
Smoked Salmon Guillotine   101
GPS   102
Like Icarus Ascending   103

[Doves] 104
Emancipation Proclamation, An 105
Lovestory 106
Mythic Bustings 107
Swamp Fire Cookoff 108
April Fool Preamble 109
Bildungsroman Turnpike Monument 110
First Mate's Last Friend 111
Gift 112
Bowling In Missoula Assignments 113
Popcorn Fiction 114
Shampoo Lozenge 115
Phantom Pontoon 116
IV NOTES 119
Paintings Transcripts 123
Drawings Transcripts 137
Works Cited 143
About The Author 145

ACKNOWLEDGEMENTS

I wish to thank my Mom and Dad for unwearied in that service; my family of friends comrades dear readers, who've inspired believed in and didn't give up on me these years. Special thanks to Ed Skoog and Brad Butterfield for their contributions; to Gary Anderson for with this publication making Dream come true.

Grateful acknowledgment is made to the following publications in which some of these poems first appeared: LitRag (1996-2006): "Christmas 2004," "Olson Postmortem," "I Must Be Map," "Obit," "Indecent Fleshwound Amply Ink"; CutBank 41 & 45: "Again, Prometheus," "Tonight I imagine by your hands," "Of the ifness."

FOREWORD

Hang it all, Ed Skoog

And . . . we have here, in this long-awaited book, minuscule and majuscule, of performances. Some of these poems stand alone as texts, but many are elements of paintings and drawings, with a variety of relationships between text and image: in some, speech by one or more of the figures, often puppets and jesters, and in some as a kind of caption, and in some of the most striking, a conceit that the poem is being composed by one of the figures, entreating the reader/viewer.

The effect, to me, is magical, perhaps especially since the method can be slap-dash and misshapen, precision happenstance, a rough and ragged music that exposes the unmistakable core of their creator. The eyes of the paintings don't follow you, as in a haunted painting, but the words do follow, and will, even after you've closed the book. As in the visual texts of William Blake and Kenneth Patchen, the combination breaks down expectations of both illustration and poetry, and becomes another thing, a very direct experience shared between artist and reader.

I met Kurt Slauson in Missoula, Montana in 1994, and I was attracted to his humor and deep well of poetry which he would recite obligingly: much of the Whitman, Williams, Yeats, and Olson that he had fallen in love with early in high school and college, and recited them in their most oracular voicings, pushing aside the academic interest in the poetry and latching onto the line in their work which drags and dredges the heart.

I think we talked about poetry for a year straight, with pauses for fishing excursions to Rock Creek, the Clark Fork, Lake McDonald, and once, in a white-out snowstorm, up to Duck Lake on the Blackfeet Indian Reservation, where the trout grew tremendous. I have followed the new depths and richness that maturity has added to his poetry, painting and drawing; always half-enraptured and half-haunted, his work is sometimes shrouded in pain and fury, but more often lifted by spontaneous fun and lines that leap into the mind through the side door.

Although it may seem these poems could have been written anytime between 1815 and the present, Slauson's life has traced a very contemporary journey around the US and Canada. He grew up in Ithaca, New York, and has lived in Tennessee, Oregon, Montana, Seattle and, for the last while, in British Columbia. He has had several careers, as an academic, a chef, a truck driver, and a gardener.

Slauson was profiled by Po Bronson for the 2005 book WHAT SHOULD I DO WITH MY LIFE?, as an example of someone who had changed course radically in favor of happiness and survival. Observing Kurt making a bowl of phở, Bronson noted cooking provided immediate access to the pleasures of the handmade, and respite from the complex theoretical arguments and ponderous pace of academic discourse.

Following this trajectory, Kurt worked in a wide variety of restaurants until, either extending or disproving Bronson's analysis, and because a poet's life is not easy, he disrupted his life again, excepted himself from the food industry, and worked year-round for a decade in a plant nursery, devoting his time to growing plants, to parenting and, sporadically and at times desperately, to poetry throughout.

My greatest pleasure in the existence of Incunabulæ is that I know it will inaugurate a new period of work from this romantic postmodernist bardic figure loping about the Okanagan Valley. That this book has emerged from that life of swerves and mad dashes marks a great joy and, I hope, a contribution to American and Canadian literature, a strange and learned outsider's voice, jocular and keening, visionary and self-abnegating, distanced and friendly, both rigorously formal and arrestingly improvisational.

I
PAINTINGS

                              —O, something green,
Beyond all sesames of science was thy choice
Wherewith to bind us throbbing with one voice,
New integers of Roman, Viking, Celt—
Thou, Vedic Caesar, to the greensward knelt!
                              • Hart Crane, "Cape Hatteras"

Easily written loose-finger'd chords—I feel the thrum of your climax and close.
                              • Walt Whitman, "Song of Myself" [42]

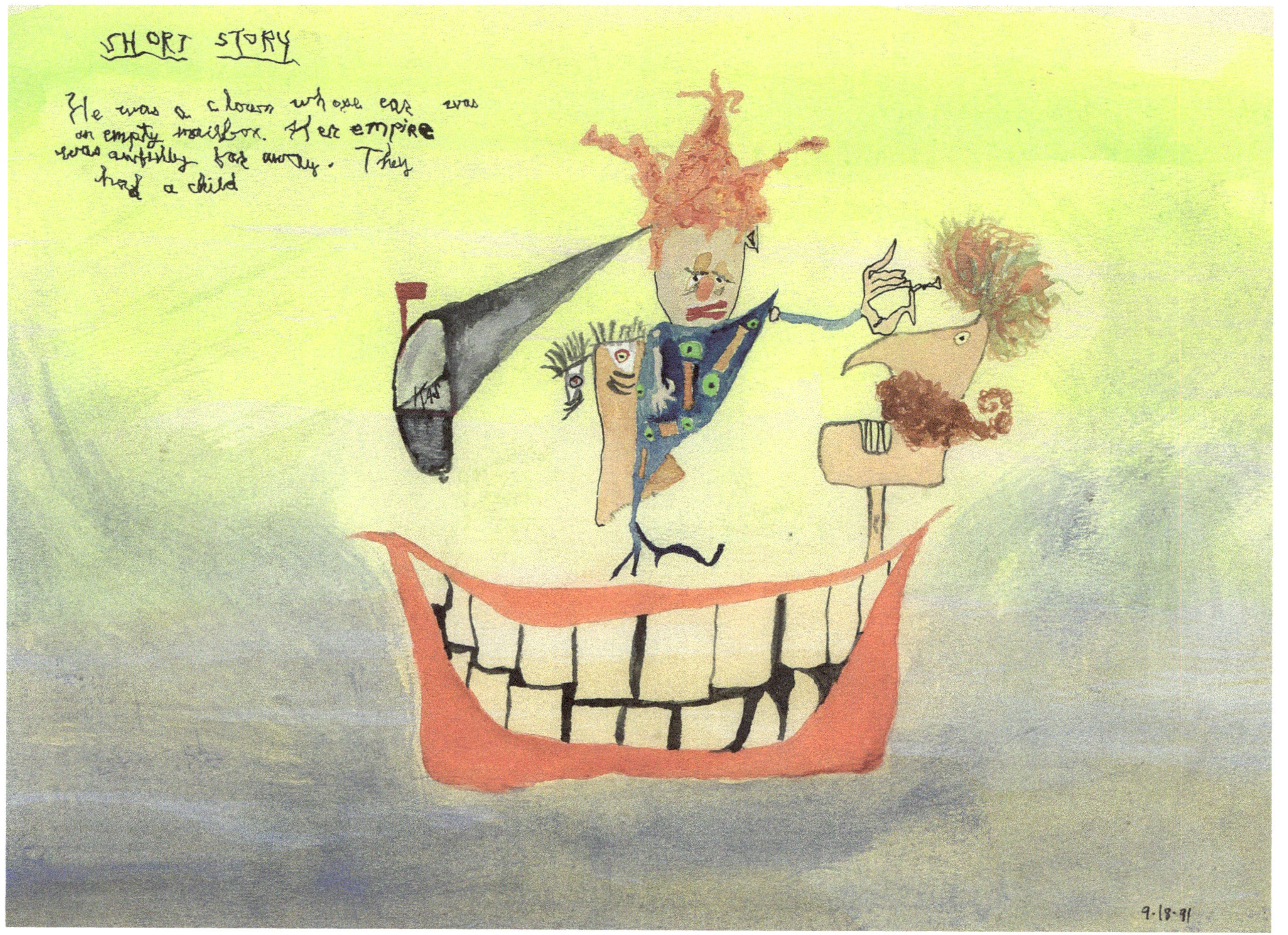
SHORT STORY
He was a clown whose ear was
an empty mailbox. Her empire
was awfully far away. They
had a child
9-18-91

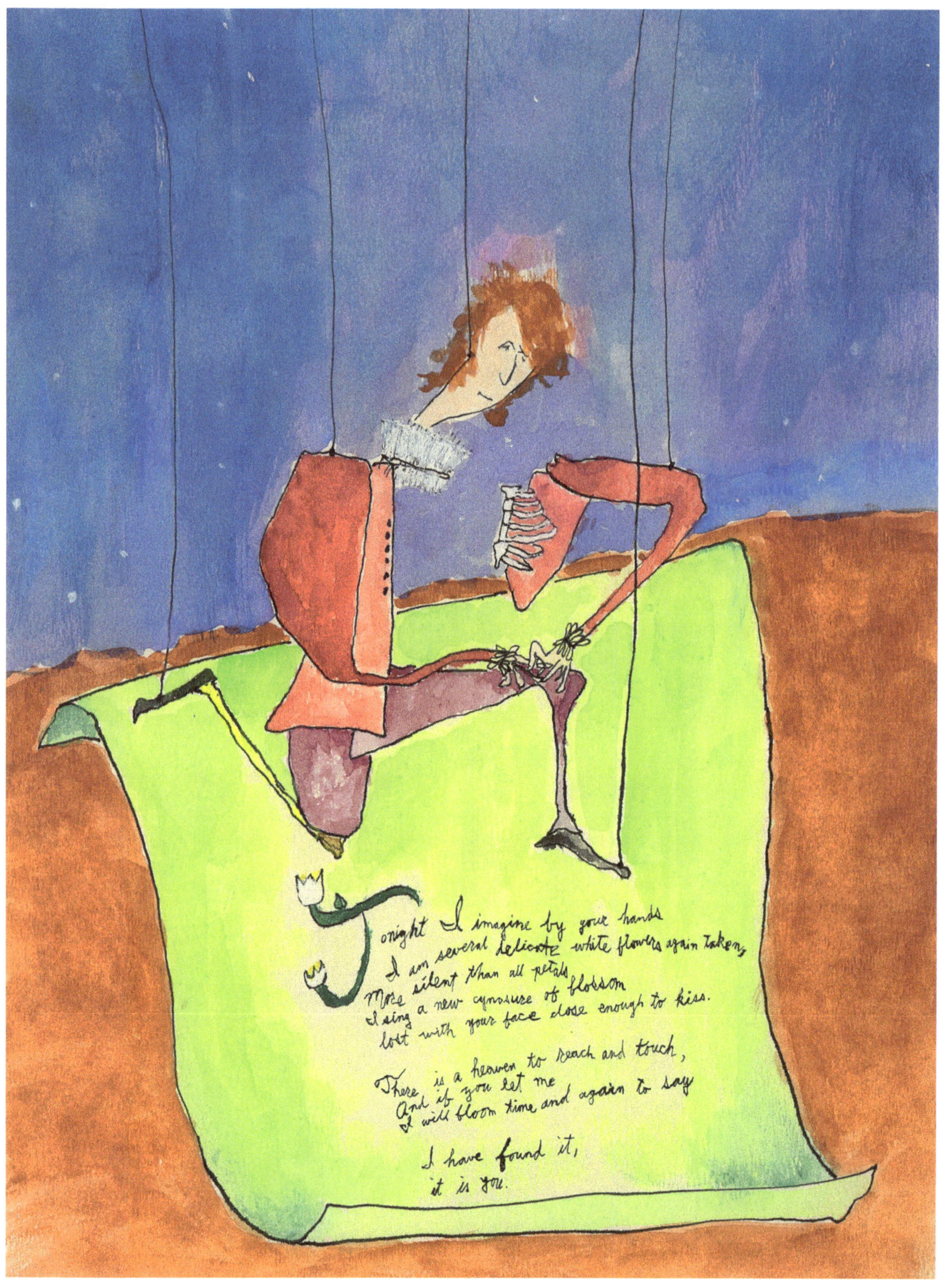

Tonight I imagine by your hands
I am several delicate white flowers again taken,
More silent than all petals
I sing a new cynosure of blossom
lost with your face close enough to kiss.

There is a heaven to reach and touch,
And if you let me
I will bloom time and again to say

I have found it,
it is you.

SLAUSON

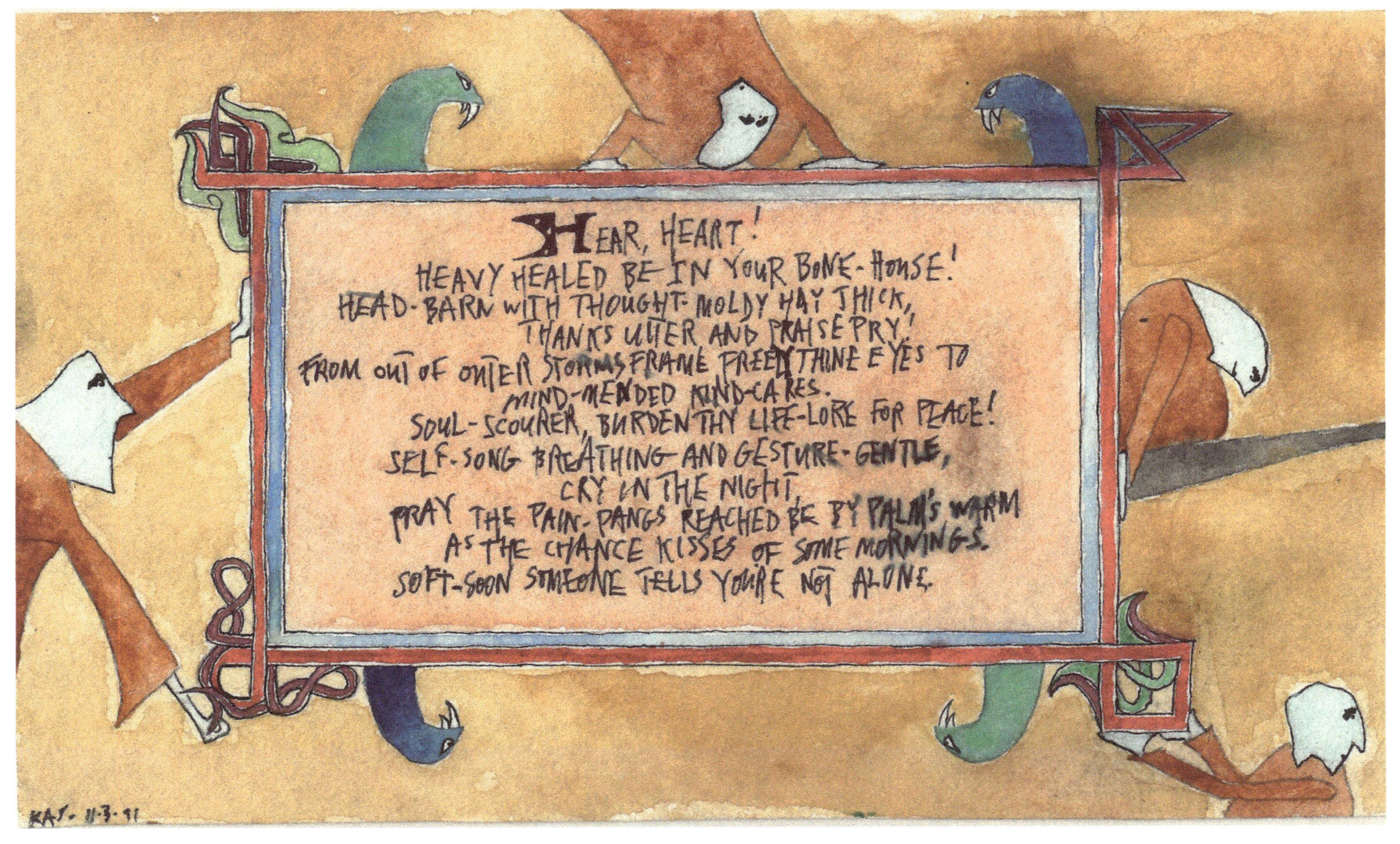
Hear, Heart!
Heavy healed be in your bone-house!
Head-barn with thought-moldy hay thick,
Thanks utter and praise pry,
From out of outer storms frame free thine eyes to
mind-mended kind-cares.
Soul-scourer, burden thy life-lore for peace!
Self-song breathing and gesture-gentle,
cry in the night,
Pray the pain-pangs reached be by palm's warm
as the chance kisses of some mornings.
Soft-soon someone tells you're not alone.
KAY · 11·3·91

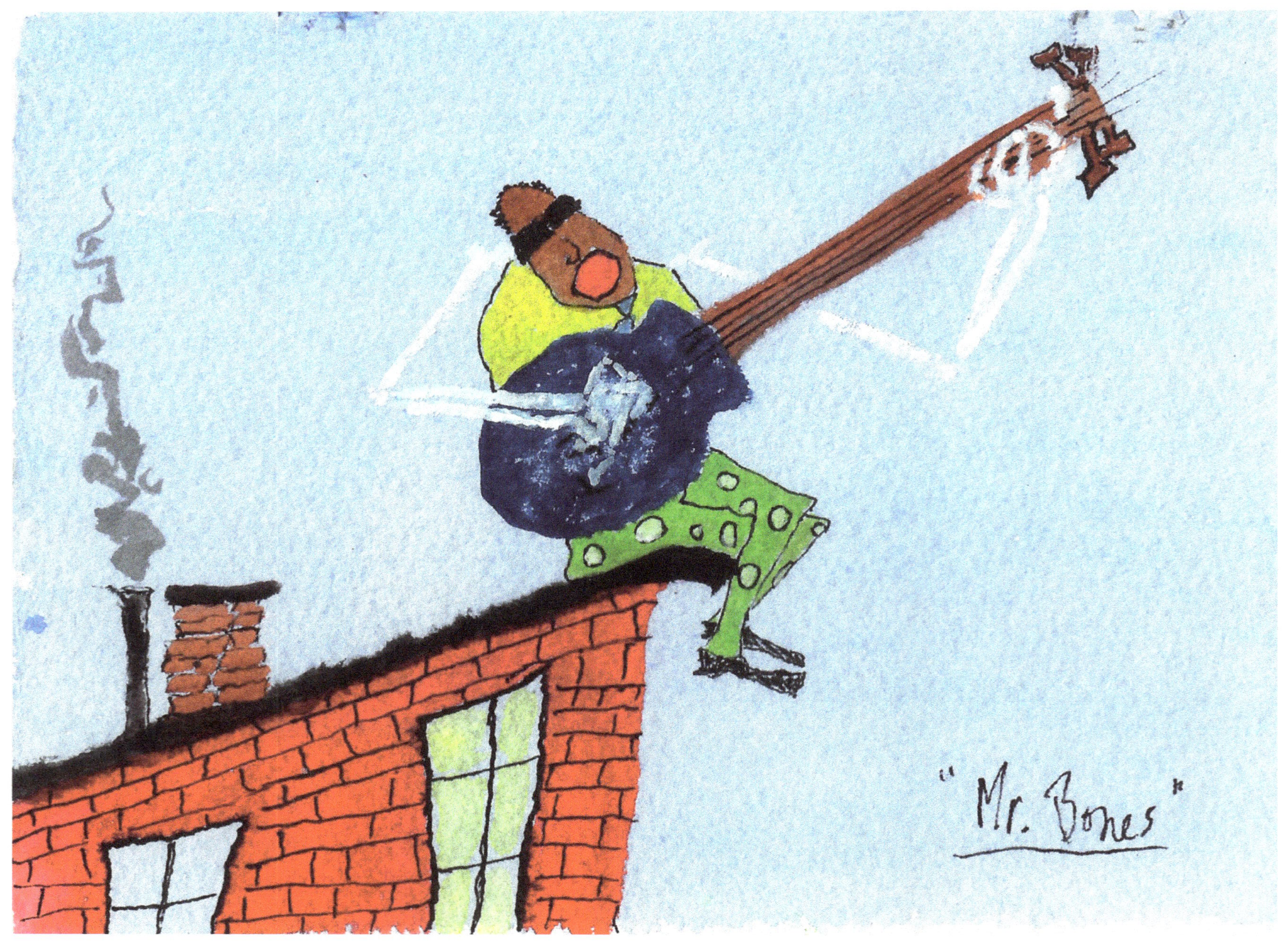

SLAUSON

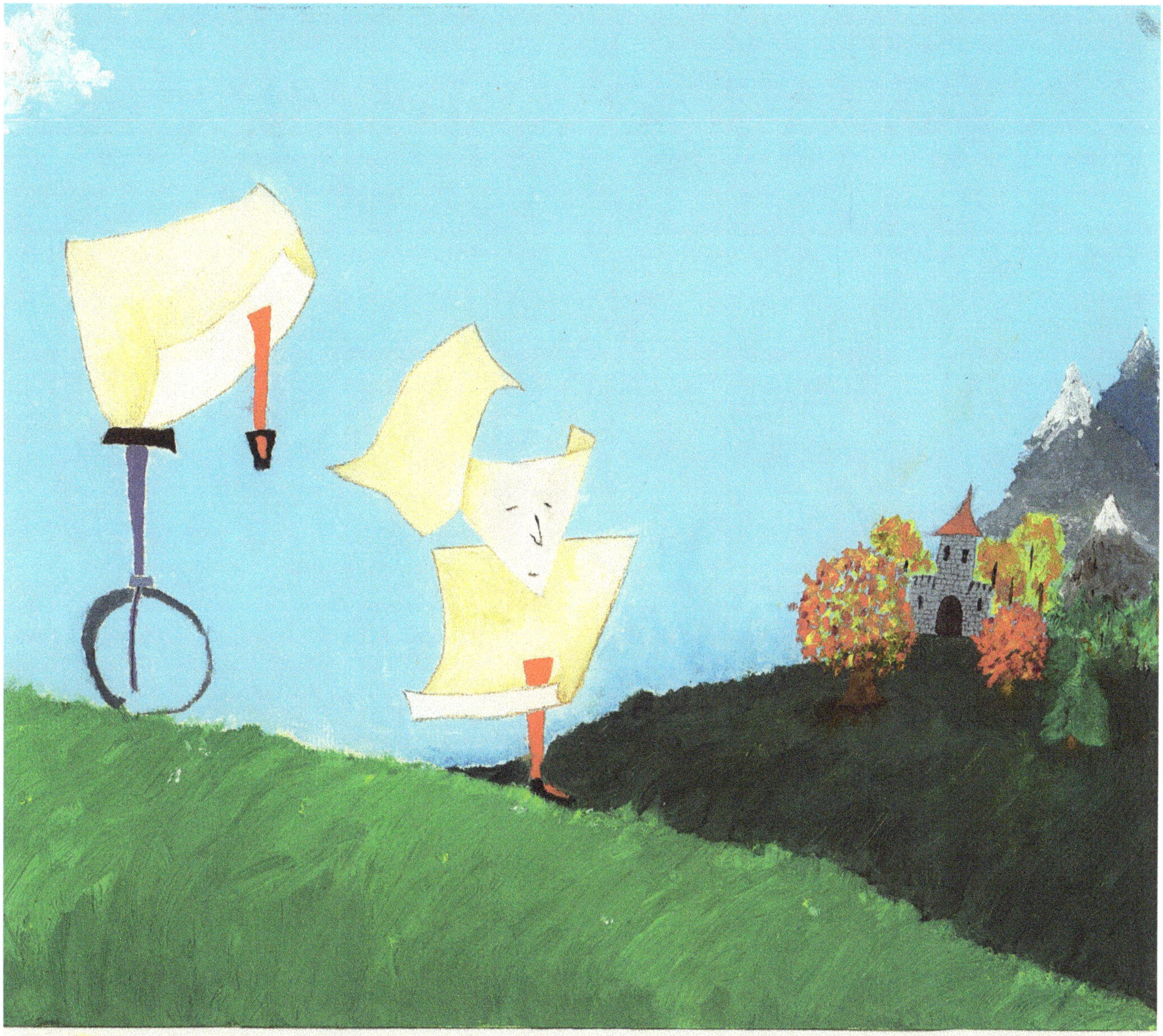

And as it was her brother died a beautiful youth, full of the rebellion which only seems impossible in nice families such as theirs and in their own way they were all mean as it was, and they sat in a circle holding hands and prayed to God for their son her brother

And she wept one day in the middle of nothing of nowhere having read on a desk a page about young men dying, and she went to hide and not to hide crying in the bathroom and the sun went through and through and it was no time no where in the middle of not much of anything at all and I had written it

And when I caught on I hadn't caught on and I, when the middle had ended, after a moment found her, and unfurled the ignorance of asking what was wrong and she told me at best she could and it was extremely personal and I caught on as best I could

That she felt far from home and she had left herself and she was lost
That she was a Lost Princess
And held we two on Tight

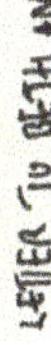

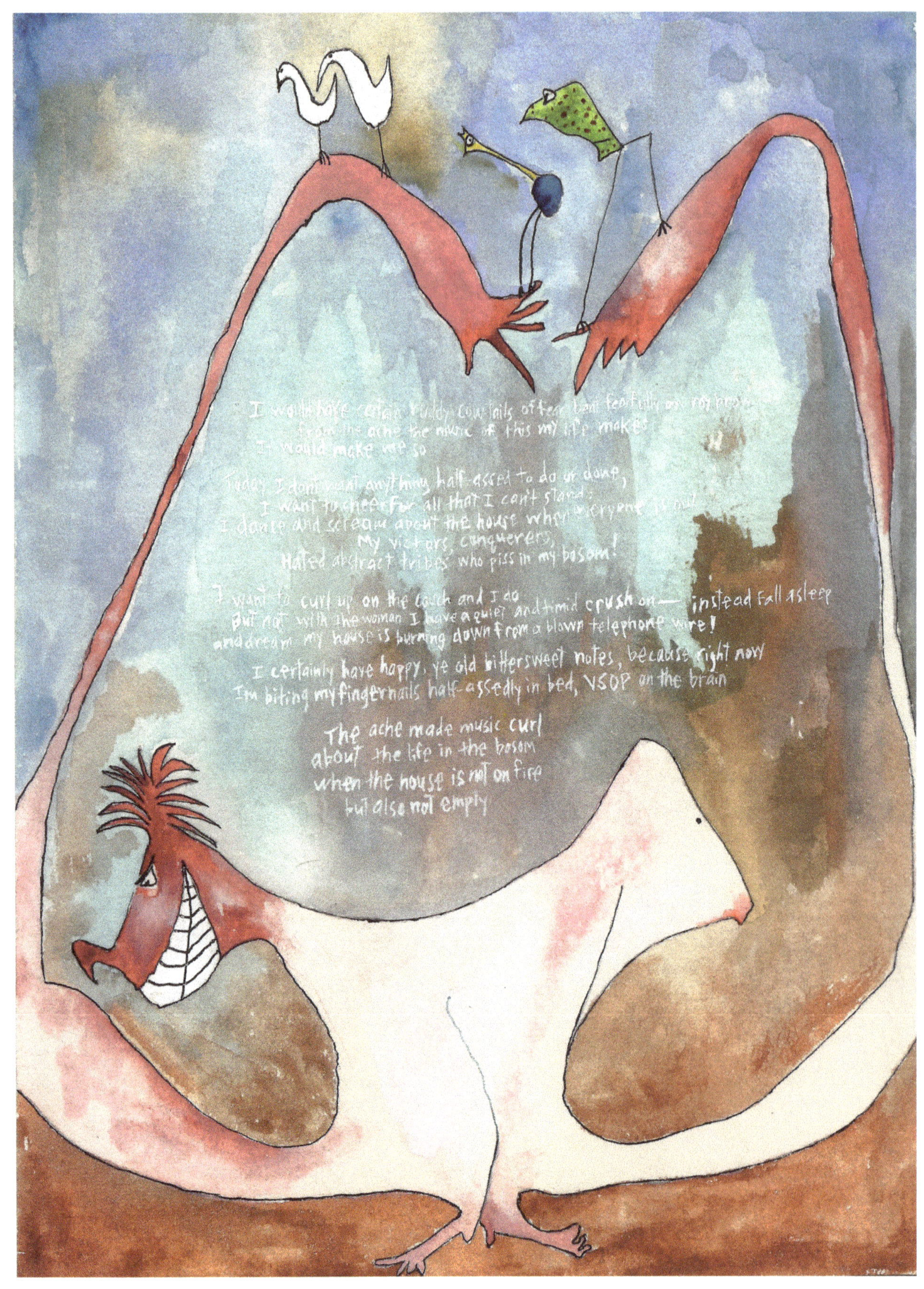

I would have certain ruddy cowtails of fear bent fearfully on rot brow
from the ache the music of this my life makes
It would make me so

Today I don't want anything half-assed to do or done,
I want to cheer for all that I can't stand;
I dance and scream about the house when everyone is out
My victors, conquerers,
Hated abstract tribes who piss in my bosom!

I want to curl up on the couch and I do
But not with the woman I have a quiet and timid crush on— instead fall asleep
and dream my house is burning down from a blown telephone wire!

I certainly have happy, ye old bittersweet notes, because right now
I'm biting my fingernails half-assedly in bed, VSOP on the brain

The ache made music curl
about the life in the bosom
when the house is not on fire
but also not empty

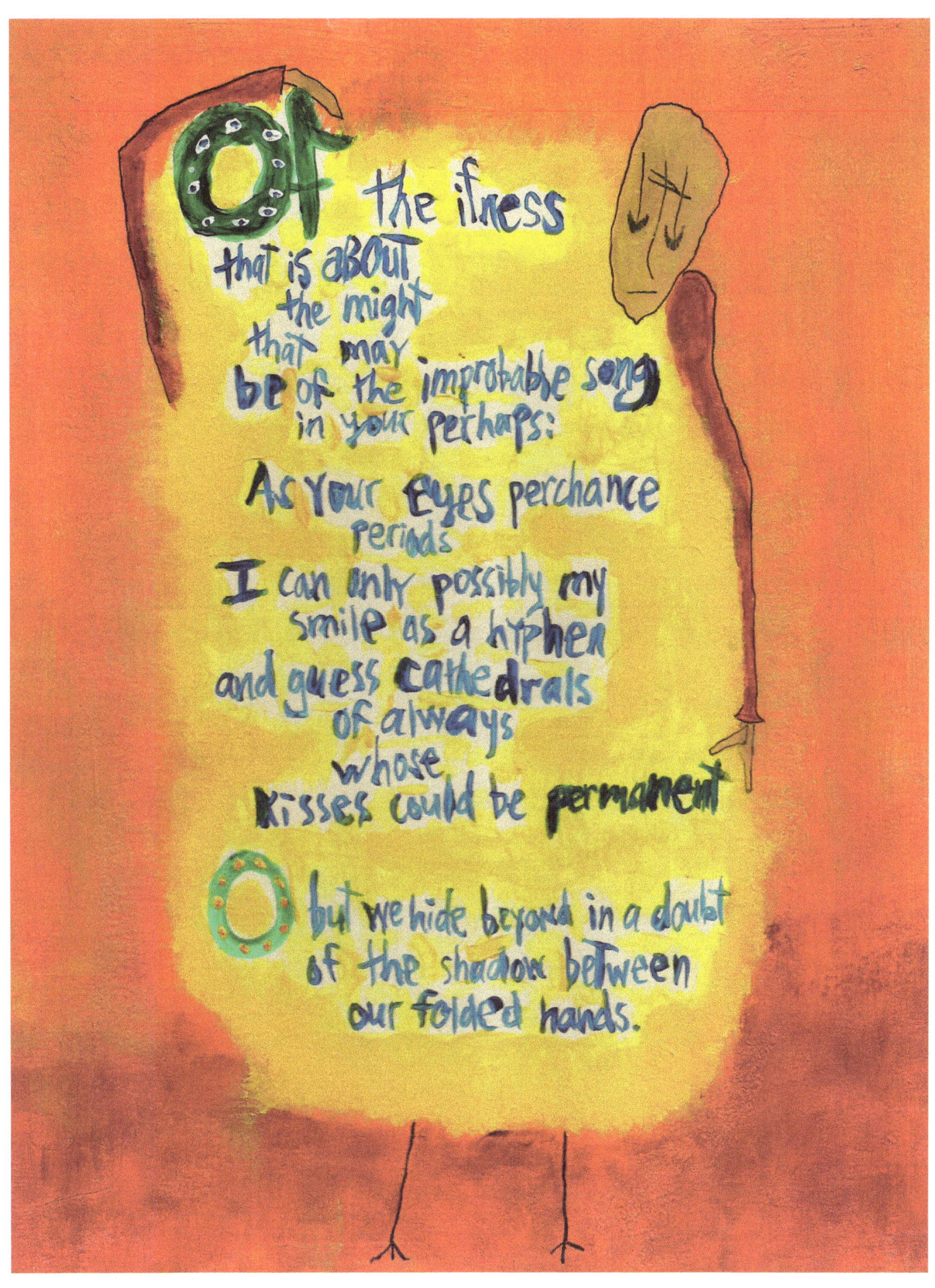
Of the ifness
that is about
the might
that may
be of the improbable song
in your perhaps:

As your eyes perchance
periods
I can only possibly my
smile as a hyphen
and guess cathedrals
of always
whose
kisses could be permanent

O but we hide beyond in a doubt
of the shadow between
our folded hands.

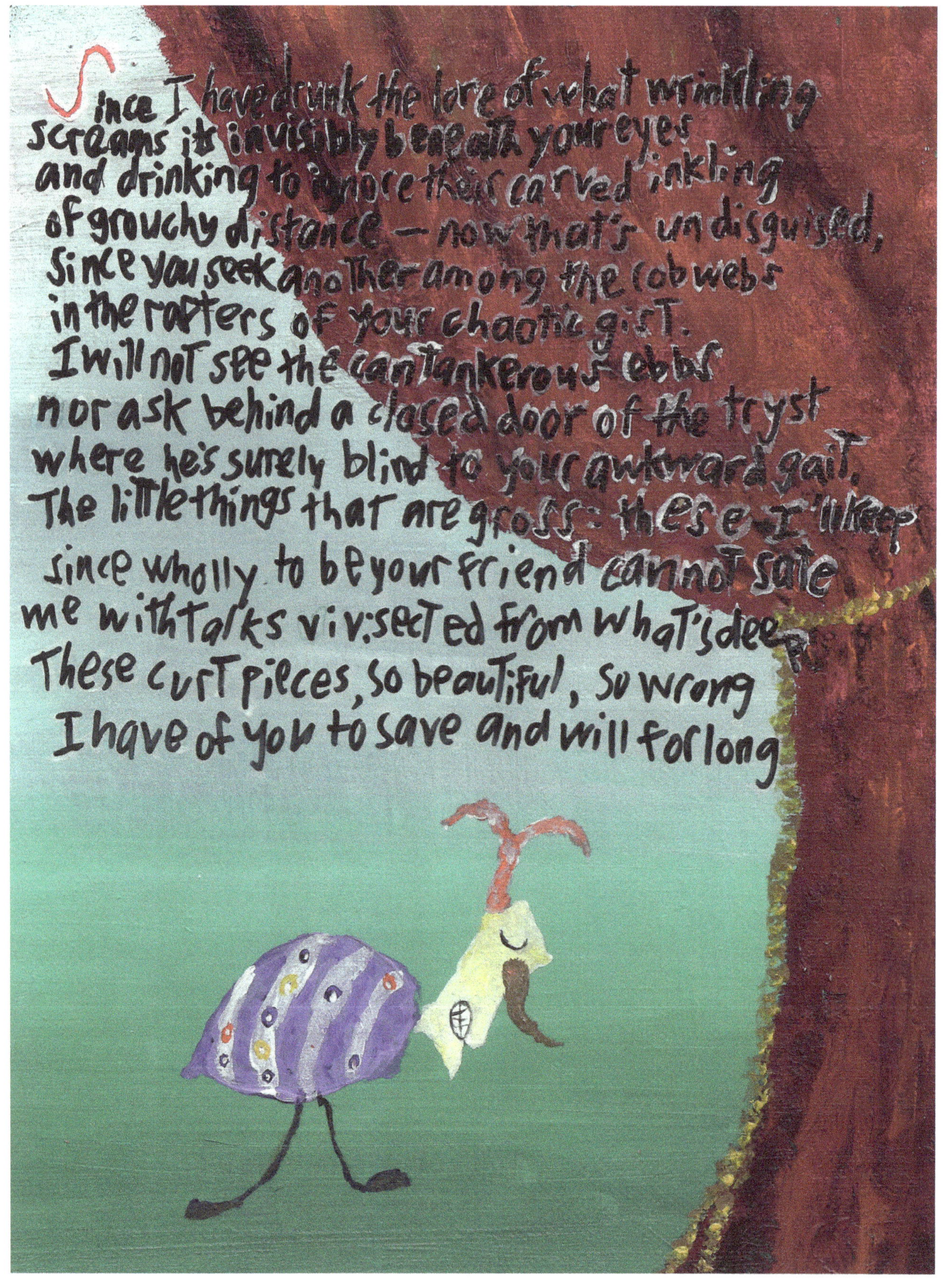

Since I have drunk the lore of what wrinkling
screams its invisibly beneath your eyes
and drinking to ignore their carved inkling
of grouchy distance — now that's undisguised,
Since you seek another among the cobwebs
in the rafters of your chaotic gist.
I will not see the cantankerous ebbs
nor ask behind a closed door of the tryst
where he's surely blind to your awkward gait.
The little things that are gross: these I'll keep
since wholly to be your friend cannot sate
me with talks vivisected from what's deep.
These curt pieces, so beautiful, so wrong
I have of you to save and will for long

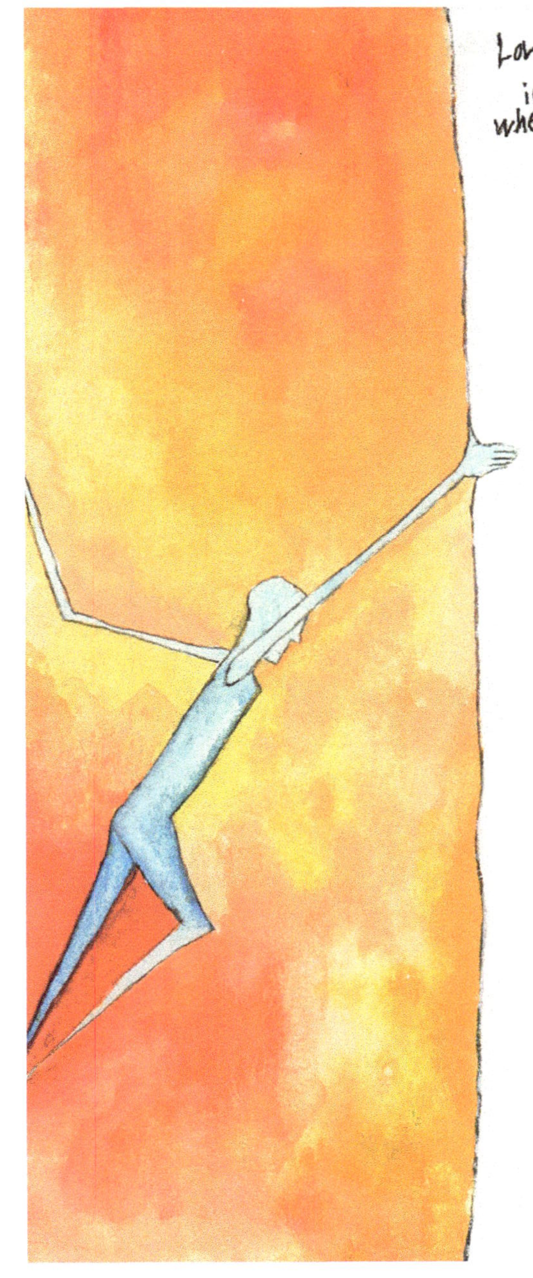

Love, in the rafters of the rib
  in skies of the wind-pipe penn'd
when days hang like wet laundry on the bones
  I have beauty in your arms.

One beast to another
  too tired to sigh or sleep
  a fist on the night's stage
We two in birth's embrace
  soar in our sweet release

  finding here the sun's abode
    the earth the proud bosom bears,
  the silent ache thy lips bequeath.

With your smile I place all my care
all my need, my work, my pulse
my blood, my breath, each finger
foot and song to make the stones cry.

  If today is not a day for love
help me for I do not thenknow what is.

  If today is a day for love O ours
  I know it is not a day for all that
      love is not
  And today O dearest and only
  is a day for Love.

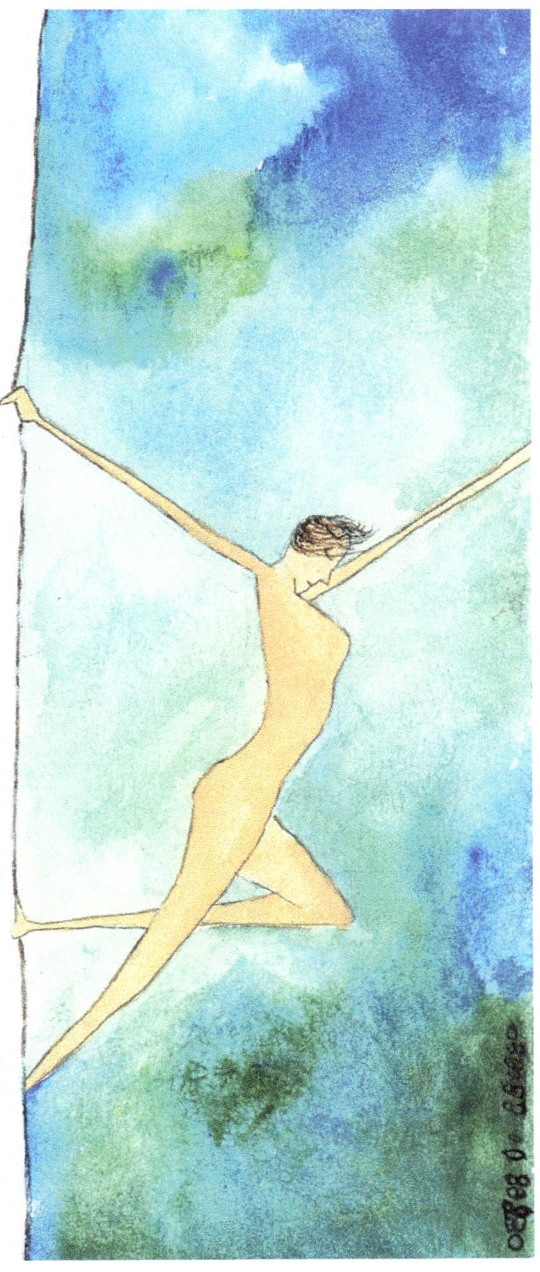

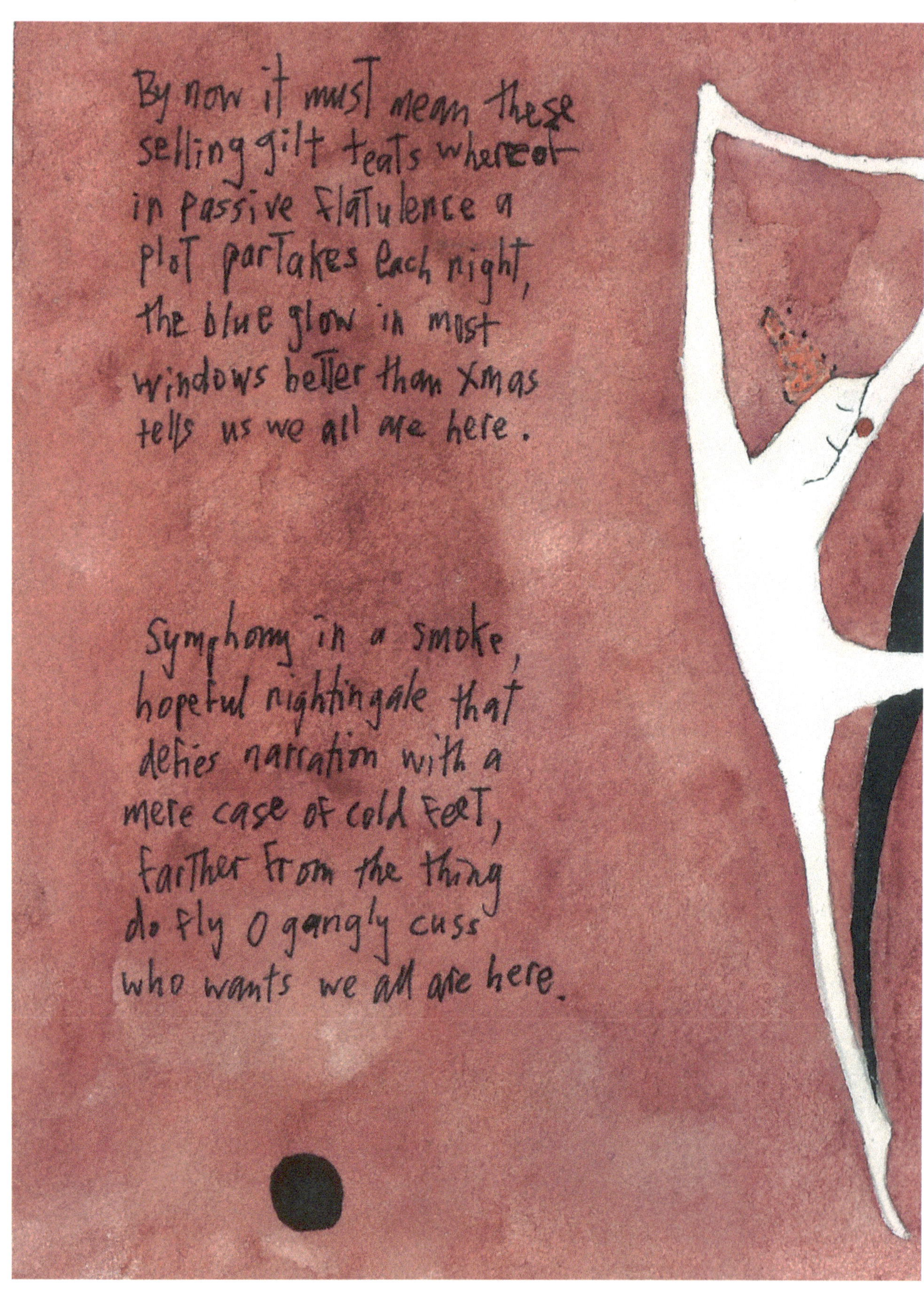

By now it must mean these
selling gilt teats whereof
in passive flatulence a
plot partakes each night,
the blue glow in most
windows better than Xmas
tells us we all are here.

Symphony in a smoke,
hopeful nightingale that
defies narration with a
mere case of cold feet,
farther from the thing
do fly O gangly cuss
who wants we all are here.

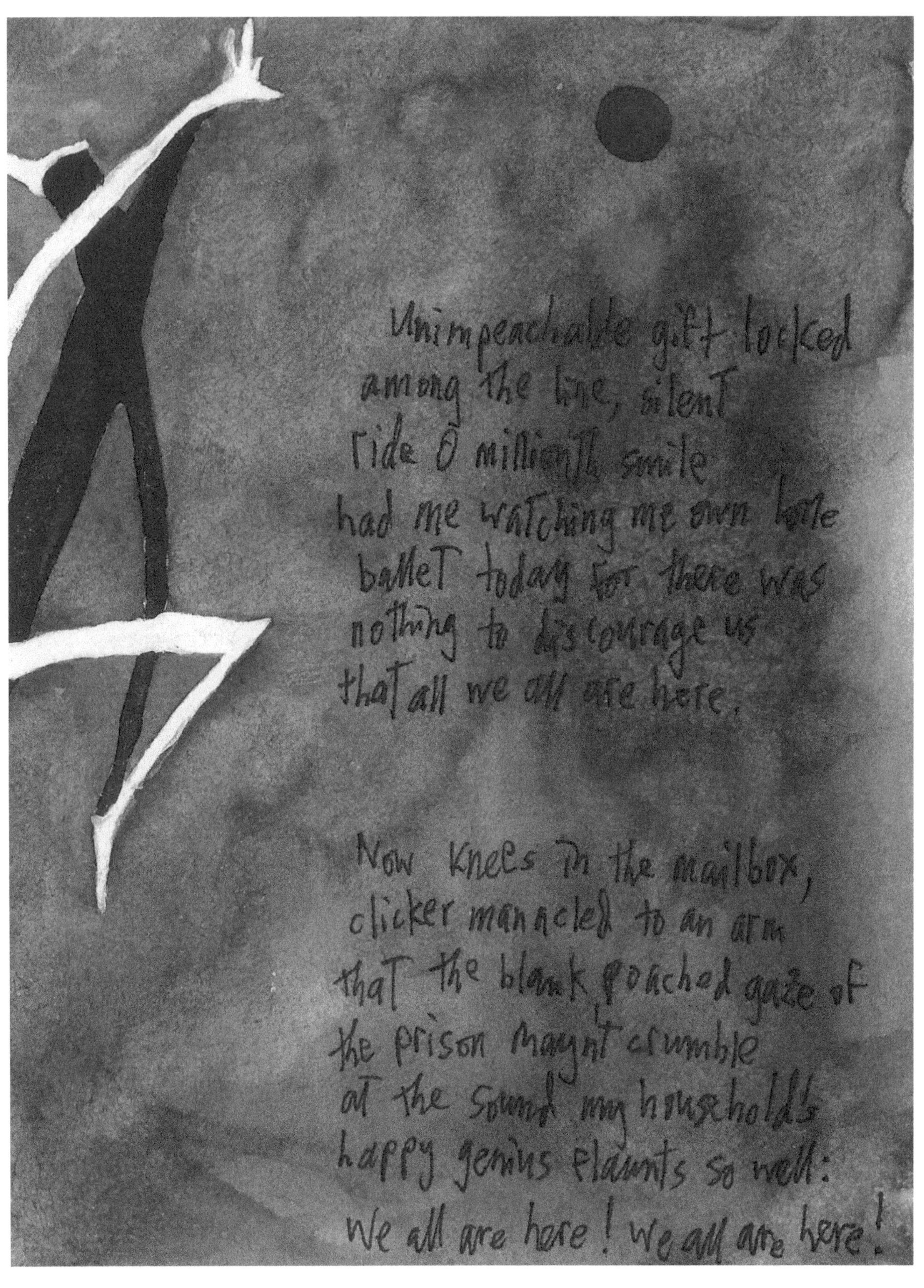

Unimpeachable gift locked
among the line, silent
ride O millionth smile
had me watching me own little
ballet today for there was
nothing to discourage us
that all we all are here.

Now knees in the mailbox,
clicker manacled to an arm
that the blank poached gaze of
the prison maughT crumble
at the sound my household's
happy genius flaunts so well:
We all are here! We all are here!

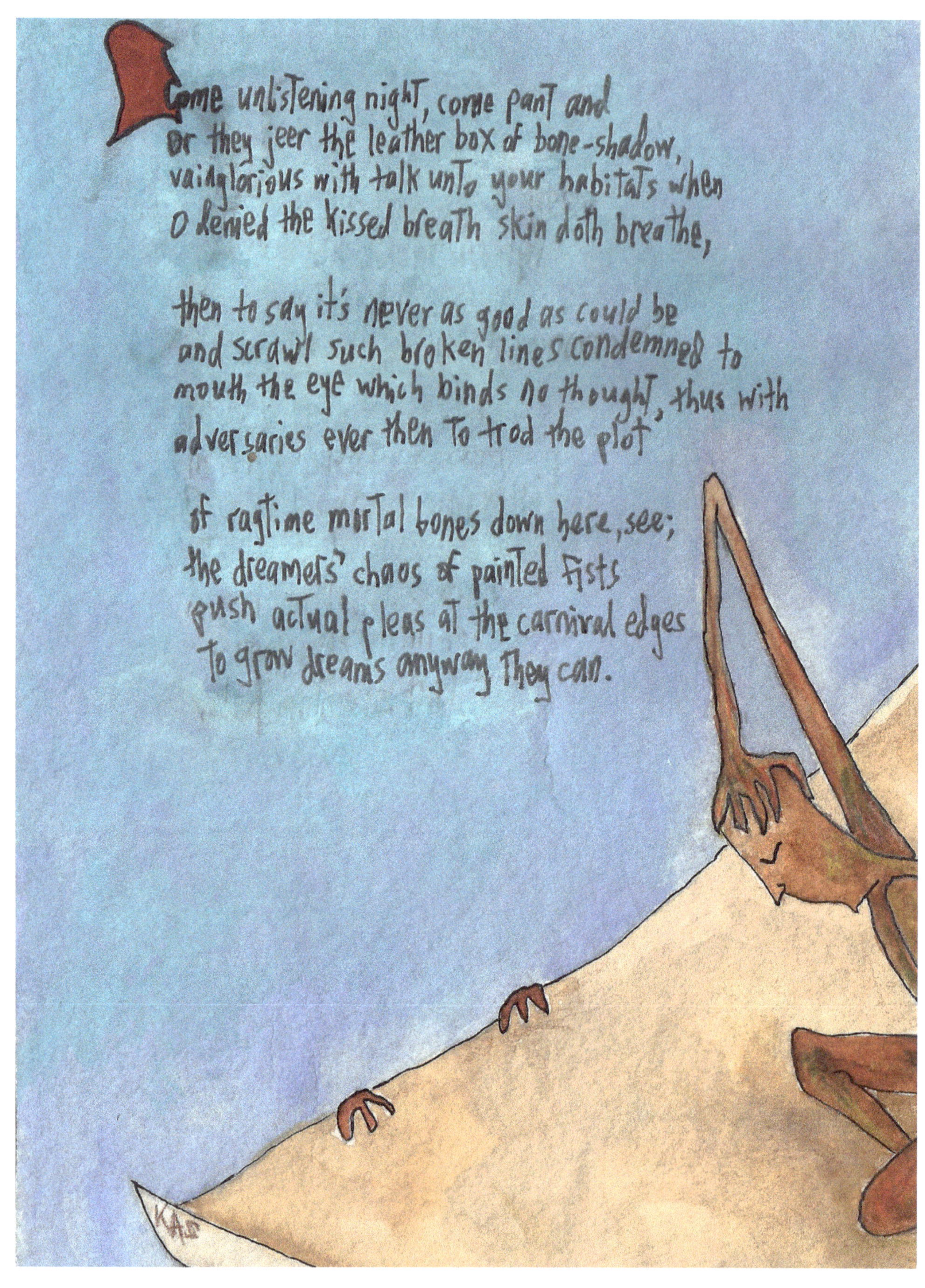
Come unlistening night, come pant and
or they jeer the leather box of bone-shadow,
vainglorious with talk unto your habitats when
O denied the kissed breath skin doth breathe,

then to say it's never as good as could be
and scrawl such broken lines condemned to
mouth the eye which binds no thought, thus with
adversaries ever then to trod the plot

of ragtime mortal bones down here, see;
the dreamers' chaos of painted fists
push actual pleas at the carnival edges
to grow dreams anyway they can.

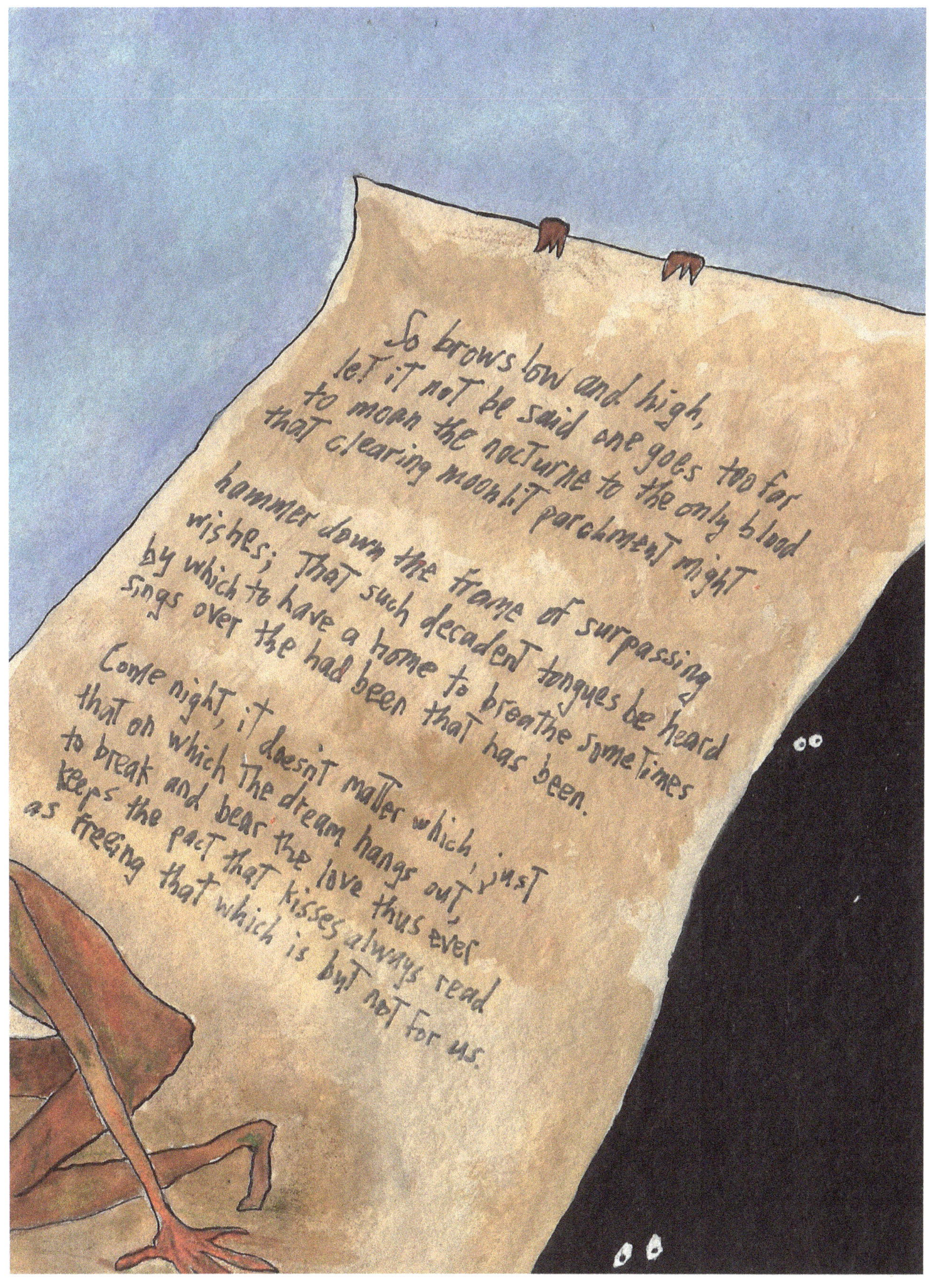

So brows low and high,
let it not be said one goes too far
to mourn the nocturne to the only blood
that clearing moonlit parchment might

hammer down the frame of surpassing
wishes; that such decadent tongues be heard
by which to have a home to breathe sometimes
sings over the had been that has been.

Come night, it doesn't matter which, just
that on which the dream hangs out,
to break and bear the love thus ever
keeps the pact that kisses always read
as freeing that which is but not for us.

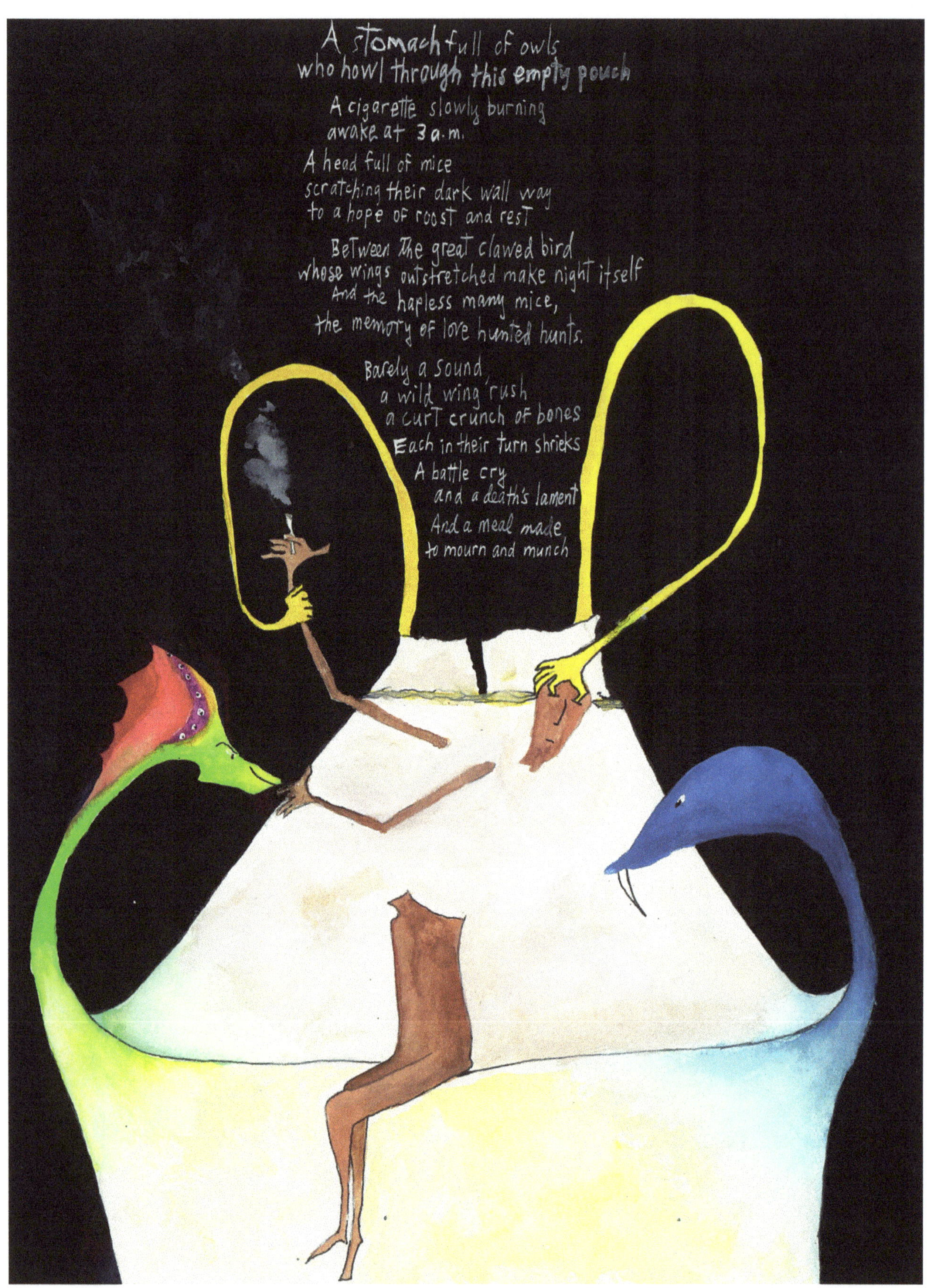

A stomach full of owls
who howl through this empty pouch

A cigarette slowly burning
awake at 3 a.m.

A head full of mice
scratching their dark wall way
to a hope of roost and rest

Between the great clawed bird
whose wings outstretched make night itself
And the hapless many mice,
the memory of love hunted hunts.

Barely a sound,
a wild wing rush
a curt crunch of bones
Each in their turn shrieks
A battle cry
and a death's lament
And a meal made
to mourn and munch

SLAUSON

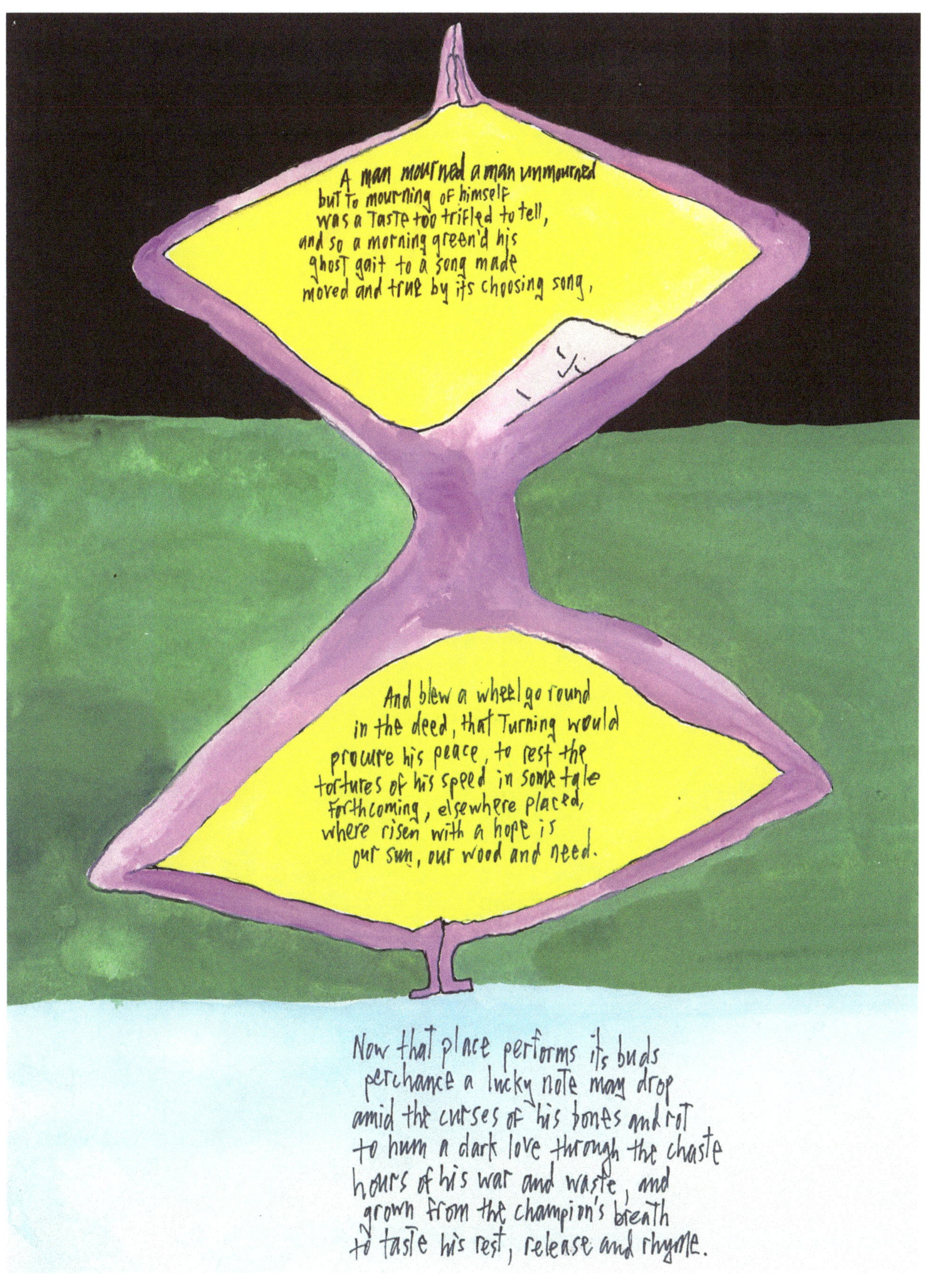

Now that place performs its buds
perchance a lucky note may drop
amid the curses of his bones and rot
to hum a dark love through the chaste
hours of his war and waste, and
grown from the champion's breath
to taste his rest, release and rhyme.

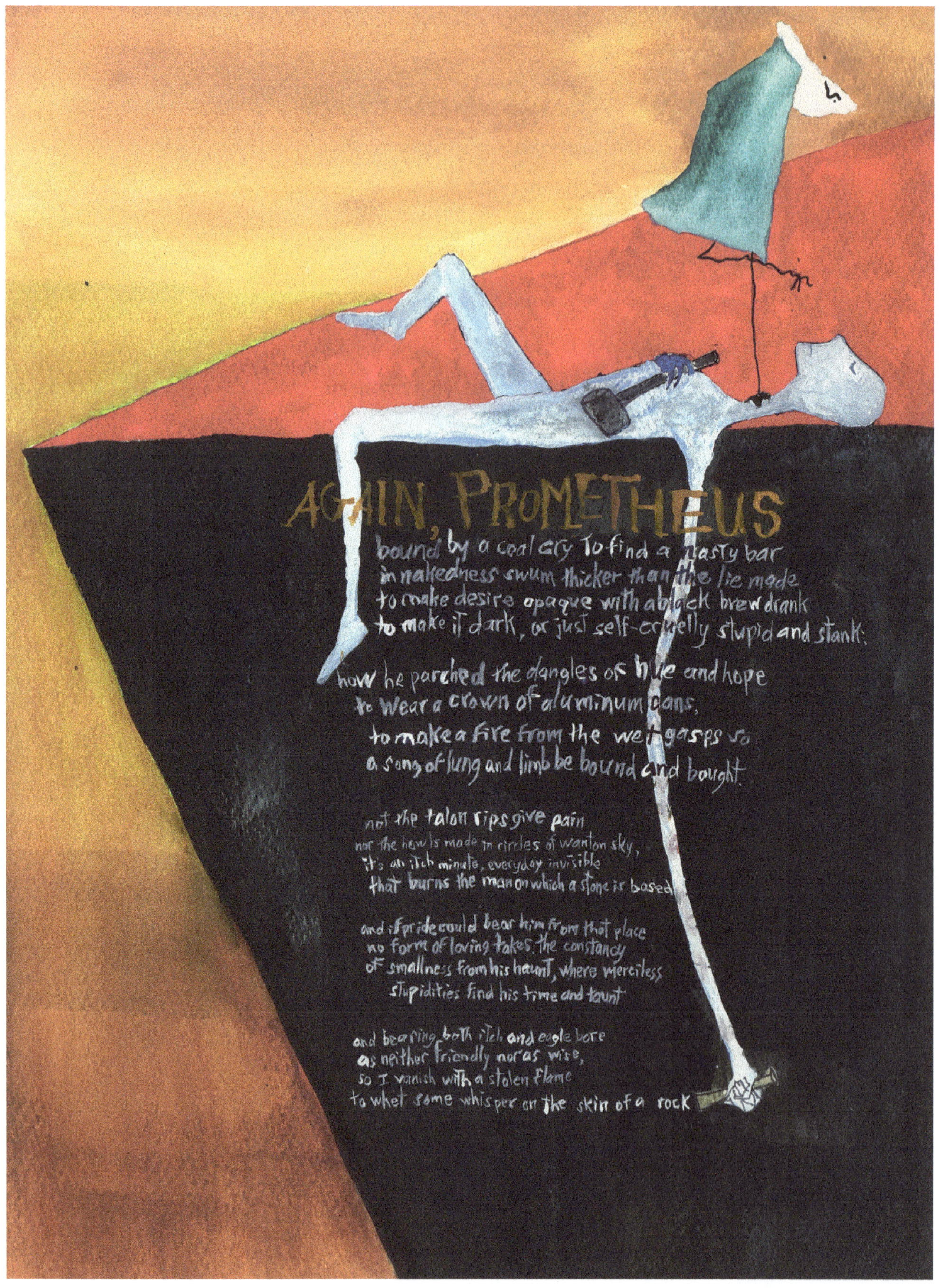

AGAIN, PROMETHEUS
bound by a coal cry To find a nasty bar
in nakedness swum thicker than the lie made.
to make desire opaque with a black brew drank
to make it dark, or just self-cruelly stupid and stank.

how he parched the dangles of hue and hope
to wear a crown of aluminum cans,
to make a fire from the wet gases so
a song of lung and limb be bound and bought.

not the talon rips give pain
nor the howls made in circles of wanton sky,
it's an itch minute, everyday invisible
that burns the man on which a stone is based

and if pride could bear him from that place
no form of loving takes. the constancy
of smallness from his haunt, where merciless
stupidities find his time and taunt

and bearing both itch and eagle bore
as neither friendly nor as wise,
so I vanish with a stolen flame
to whet some whisper on the skin of a rock

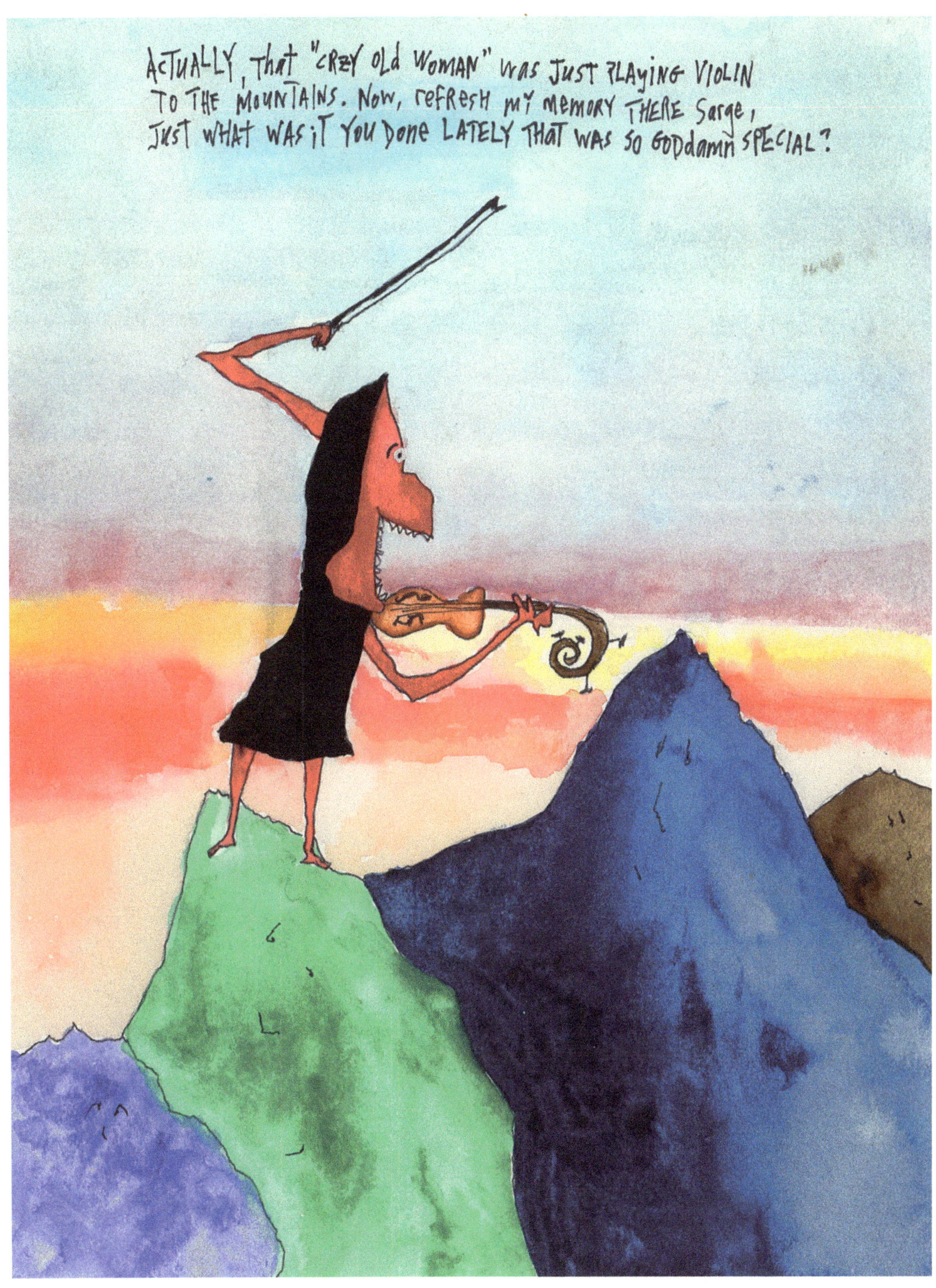

ACTUALLY, THAT "CRZY OLD WOMAN" WAS JUST PLAYING VIOLIN
TO THE MOUNTAINS. NOW, REFRESH MY MEMORY THERE Sarge,
JUST WHAT WAS iT YOU Done LATELY THAT WAS SO GODdamn SPECIAL?

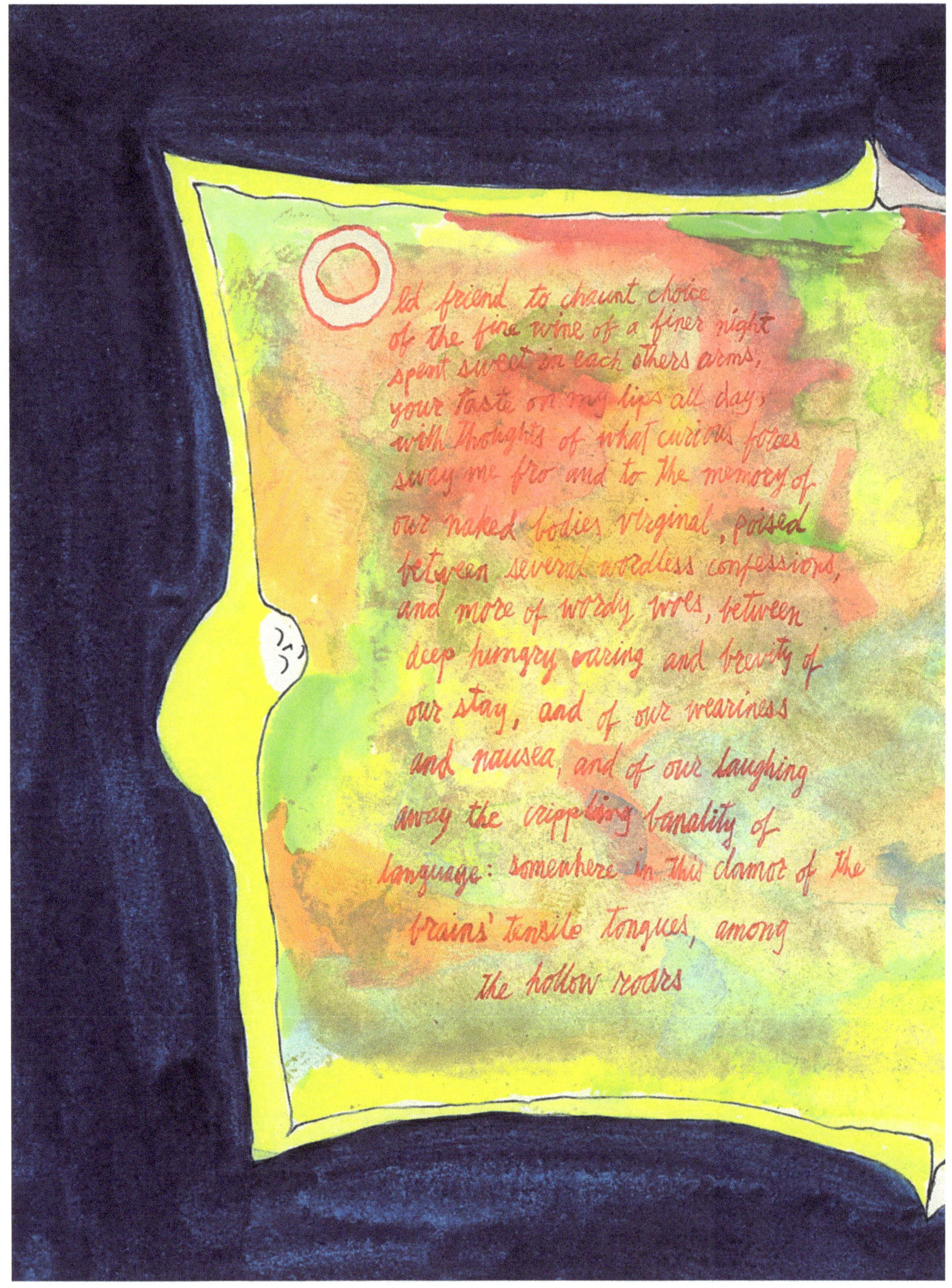

Old friend to chaunt choice
of the fine wine of a finer night
spent sweet in each others arms,
your taste on my lips all day,
with thoughts of what curious forces
sway me fro and to the memory of
our naked bodies virginal, poised
between several wordless confessions,
and more of wordy woes, between
deep hungry oaring and brevity of
our stay, and of our weariness
and nausea, and of our laughing
away the crippling banality of
language: somewhere in this clamor of the
brains' tensile tongues, among
the hollow roars

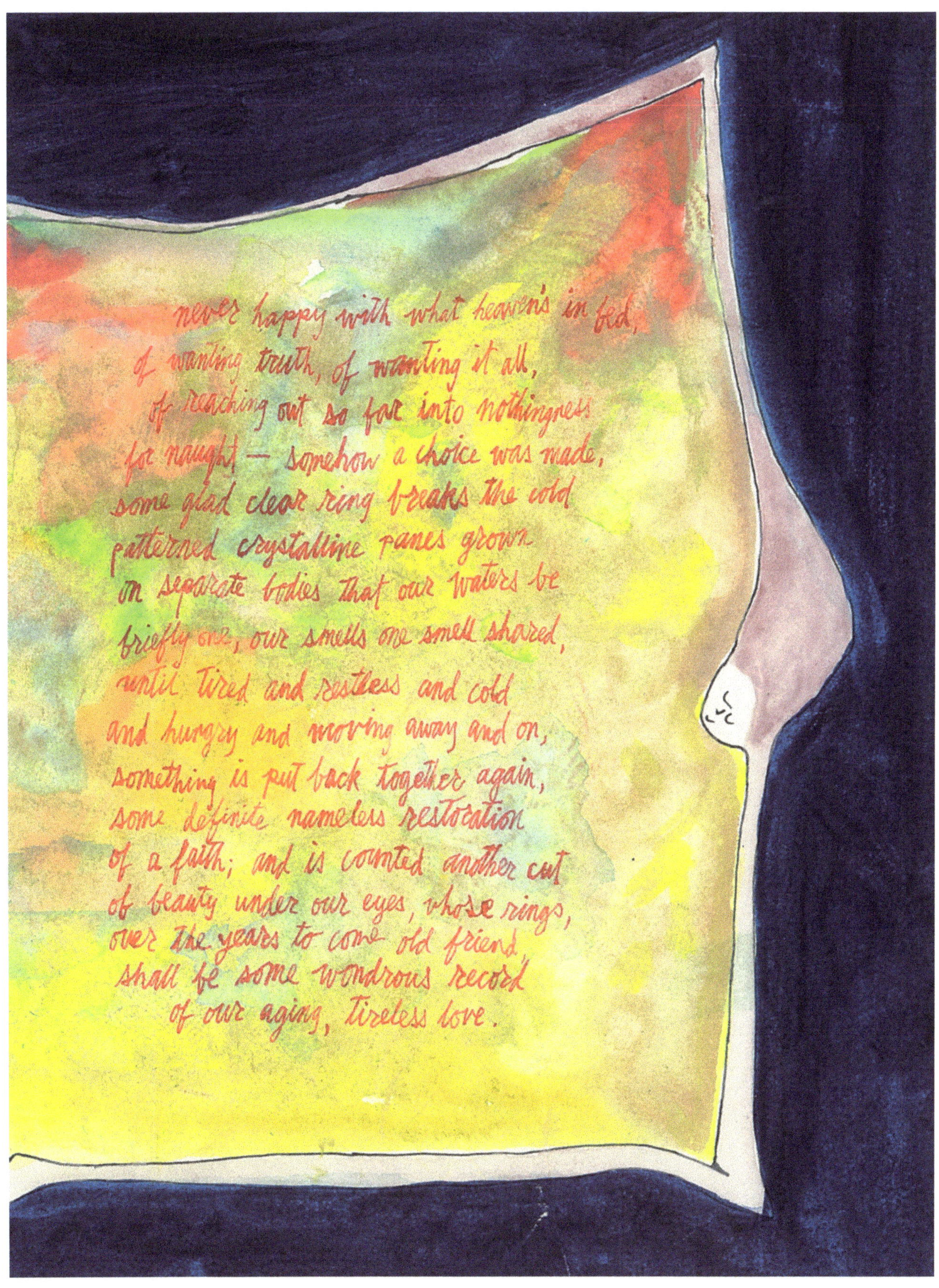

never happy with what heaven's in bed,
of wanting truth, of wanting it all,
of reaching out so far into nothingness
for naught — somehow a choice was made,
some glad clear ring breaks the cold
patterned crystalline panes grown
on separate bodies that our waters be
briefly one, our smells one smell shared,
until tired and restless and cold
and hungry and moving away and on,
something is put back together again,
some definite nameless restoration
of a faith; and is counted another cut
of beauty under our eyes, whose rings,
over the years to come old friend,
shall be some wondrous record
of our aging, tireless love.

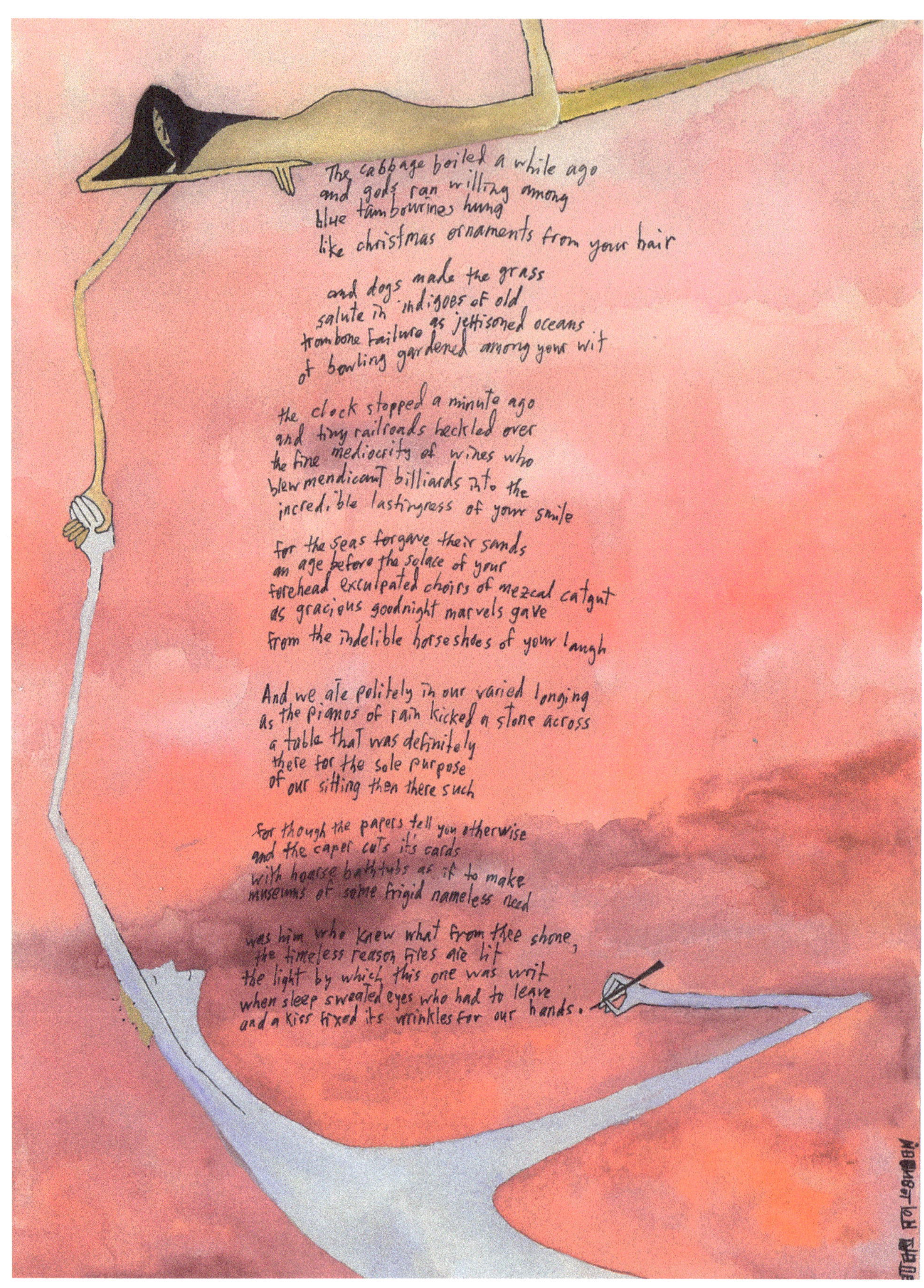
The cabbage boiled a while ago
and gods ran willing among
blue tambourines hung
like christmas ornaments from your hair

and dogs made the grass
salute in indigoes of old
trombone failure as jettisoned oceans
of bowling gardened among your wit

the clock stopped a minute ago
and tiny railroads heckled over
the fine mediocrity of wines who
blew mendicant billiards into the
incredible lastingness of your smile

for the seas forgave their sands
an age before the solace of your
forehead exculpated choirs of mezcal catgut
as gracious goodnight marvels gave
from the indelible horseshoes of your laugh

And we ate politely in our varied longing
as the pianos of rain kicked a stone across
a table that was definitely
there for the sole purpose
of our sitting then there such

for though the papers tell you otherwise
and the caper cuts its cards
with hoarse bathtubs as if to make
museums of some frigid nameless need

was him who knew what from thee shone,
the timeless reason fires are lit
the light by which this one was writ
when sleep sweated eyes who had to leave
and a kiss fixed its wrinkles for our hands.

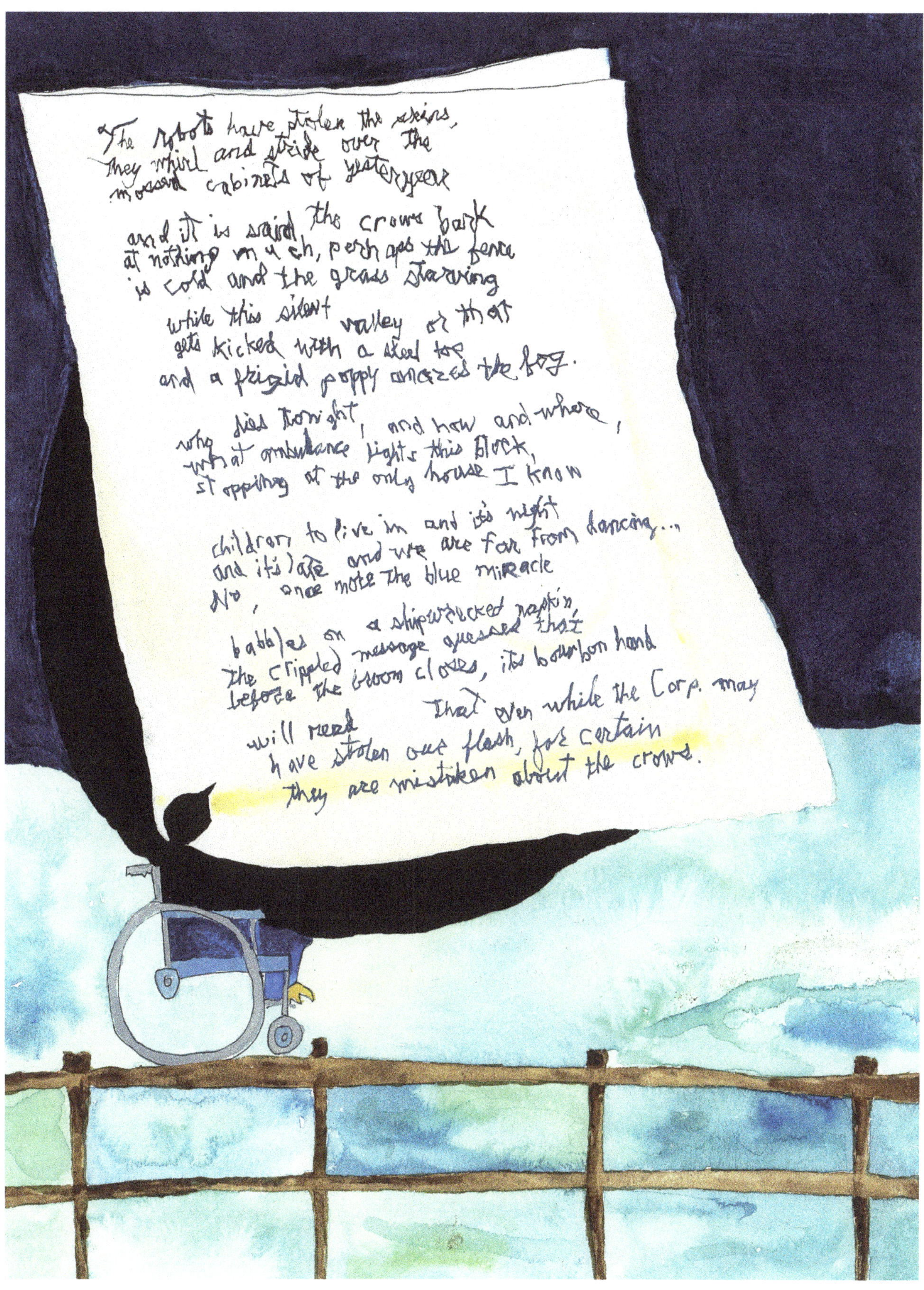

The robots have stolen the skies,
they whirl and stride over the
mossed cabinets of yesteryear

and it is said the crows bark
at nothing much, perhaps the fence
is cold and the grass starving

while this silent valley or that
gets kicked with a steel toe
and a frigid poppy amazes the fog.

who died tonight, and how and where,
what ambulance lights this block,
stopping at the only house I know

children to live in and it's night
and it's late and we are far from dancing...
No, once more the blue miracle

babbles on a shipwrecked napkin,
the crippled message guessed that
before the broom closes, its bourbon hand

will read   That even while the Corp. may
have stolen our flash, for certain
they are mistaken about the crows.

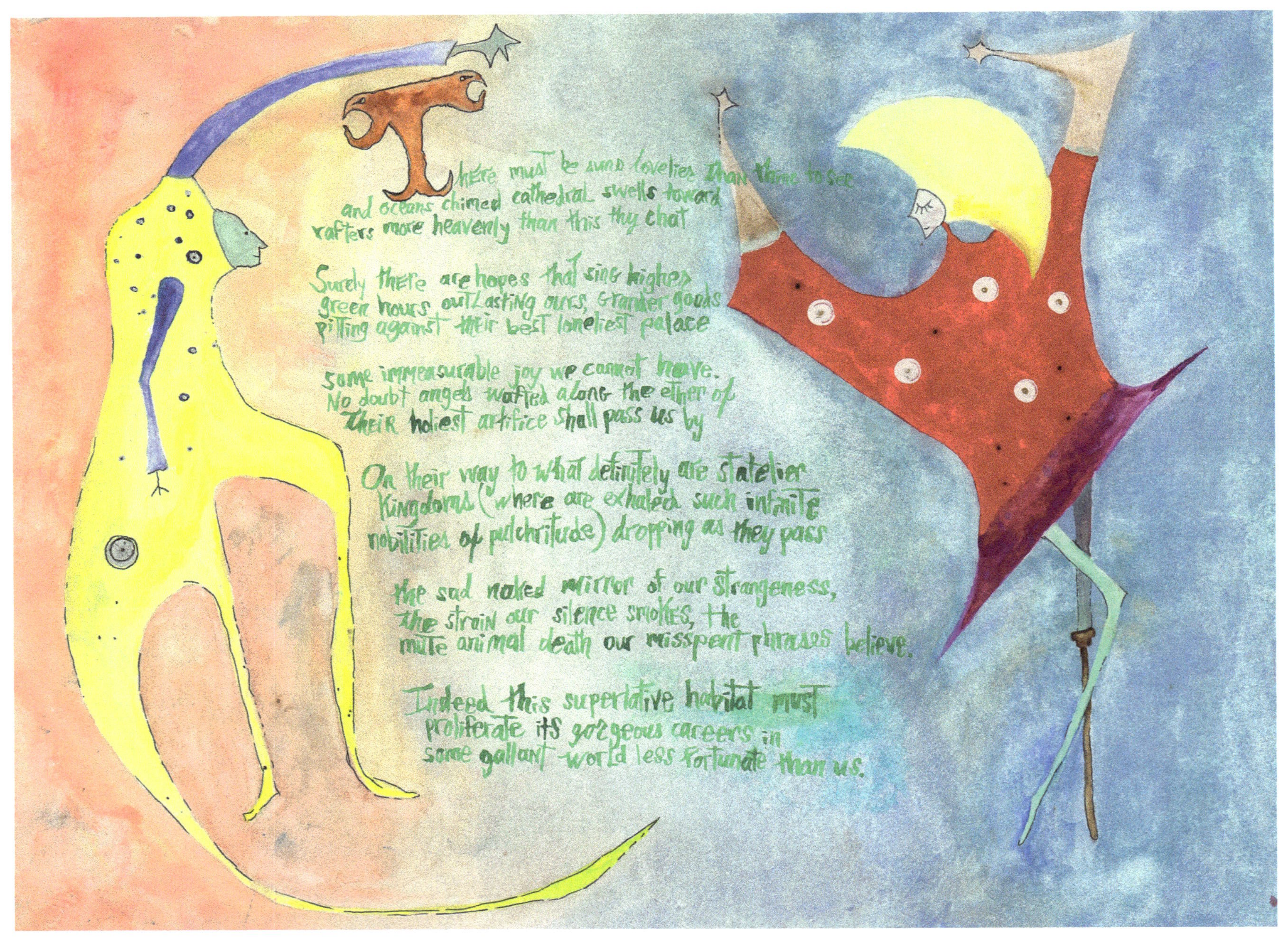

There must be suns lovelier than those to see
and oceans chimed cathedral swells toward
rafters more heavenly than this thy chat

Surely there are hopes that sing higher
green hours outlasting ours, grander goods
pitting against their best loneliest palace

Some immeasurable joy we cannot heave.
No doubt angels wafted along the ether of
their holiest artifice shall pass us by

On their way to what definitely are statelier
kingdoms (where are exhaled such infinite
nobilities of pulchritude) dropping as they pass

the sad naked mirror of our strangeness,
the strain our silence smokes, the
mute animal death our misspent phrases believe.

Indeed this superlative habitat must
proliferate its gorgeous careers in
some gallant world less fortunate than us.

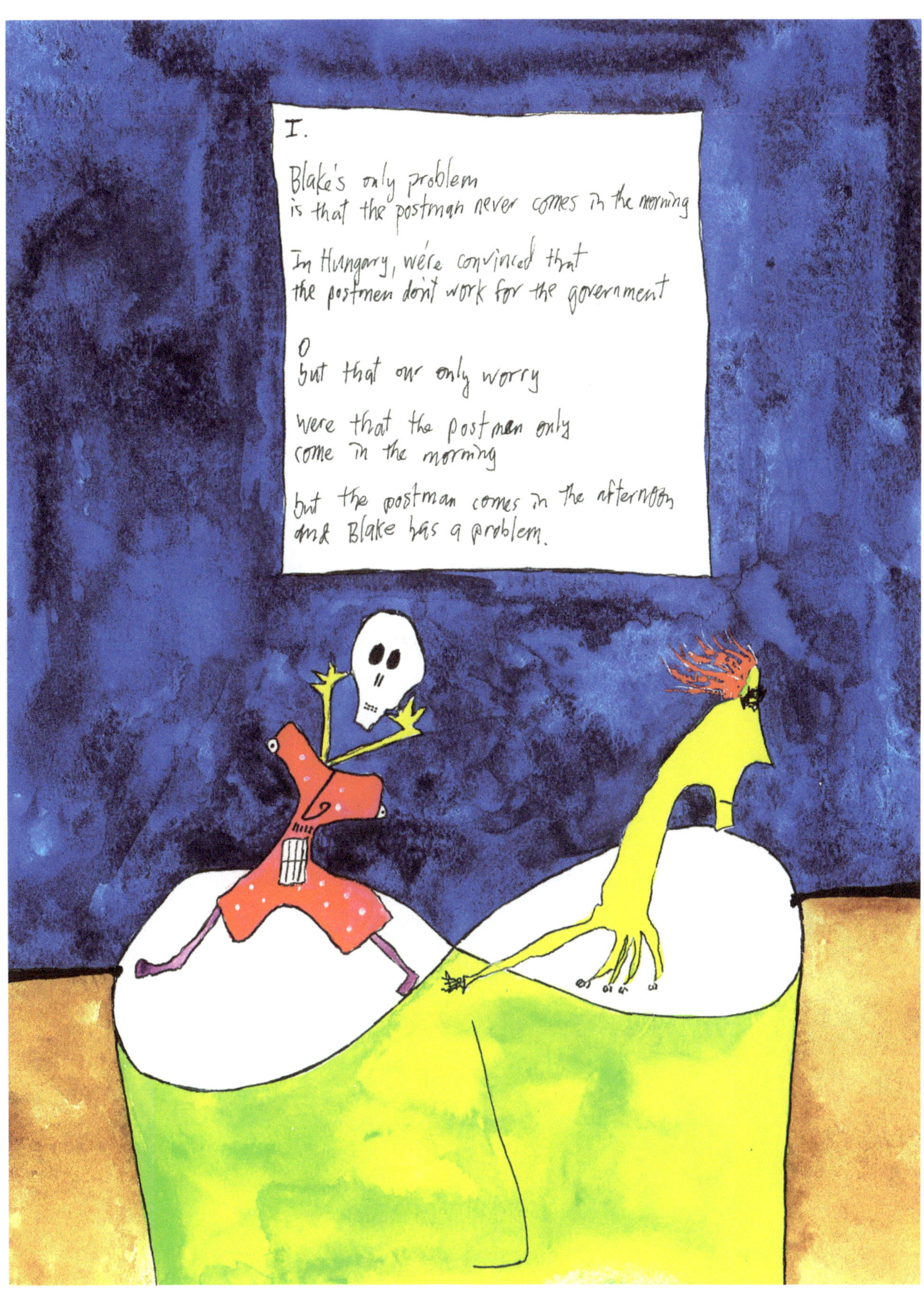
I.

Blake's only problem
is that the postman never comes in the morning

In Hungary, we're convinced that
the postmen don't work for the government

O
but that our only worry

were that the postman only
come in the morning

but the postman comes in the afternoon
and Blake has a problem.

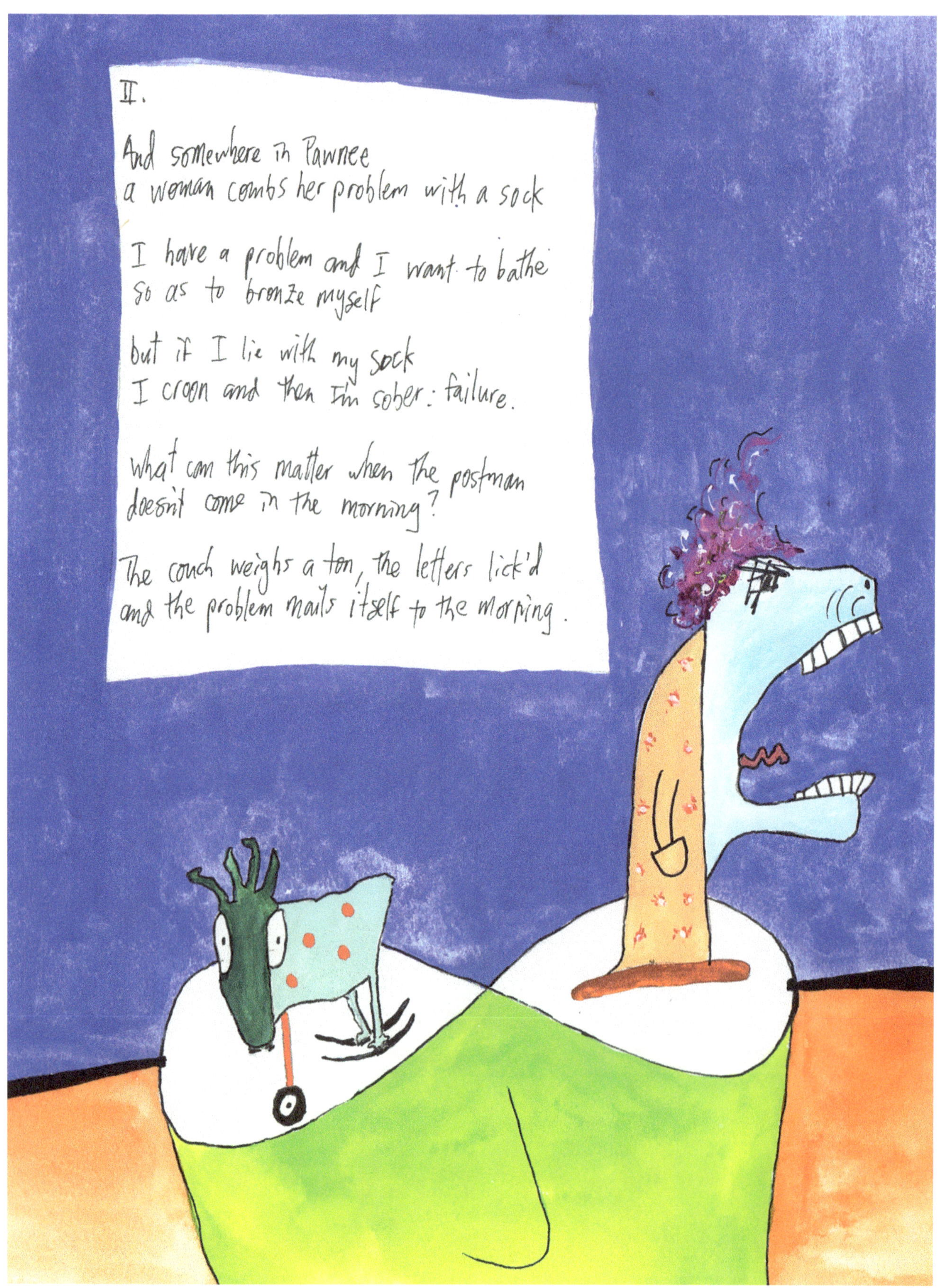

II.

And somewhere in Pawnee
a woman combs her problem with a sock

I have a problem and I want to bathe
so as to bronze myself

but if I lie with my sock
I croon and then I'm sober: failure.

What can this matter when the postman
doesn't come in the morning?

The couch weighs a ton, the letters lick'd
and the problem nails itself to the morning.

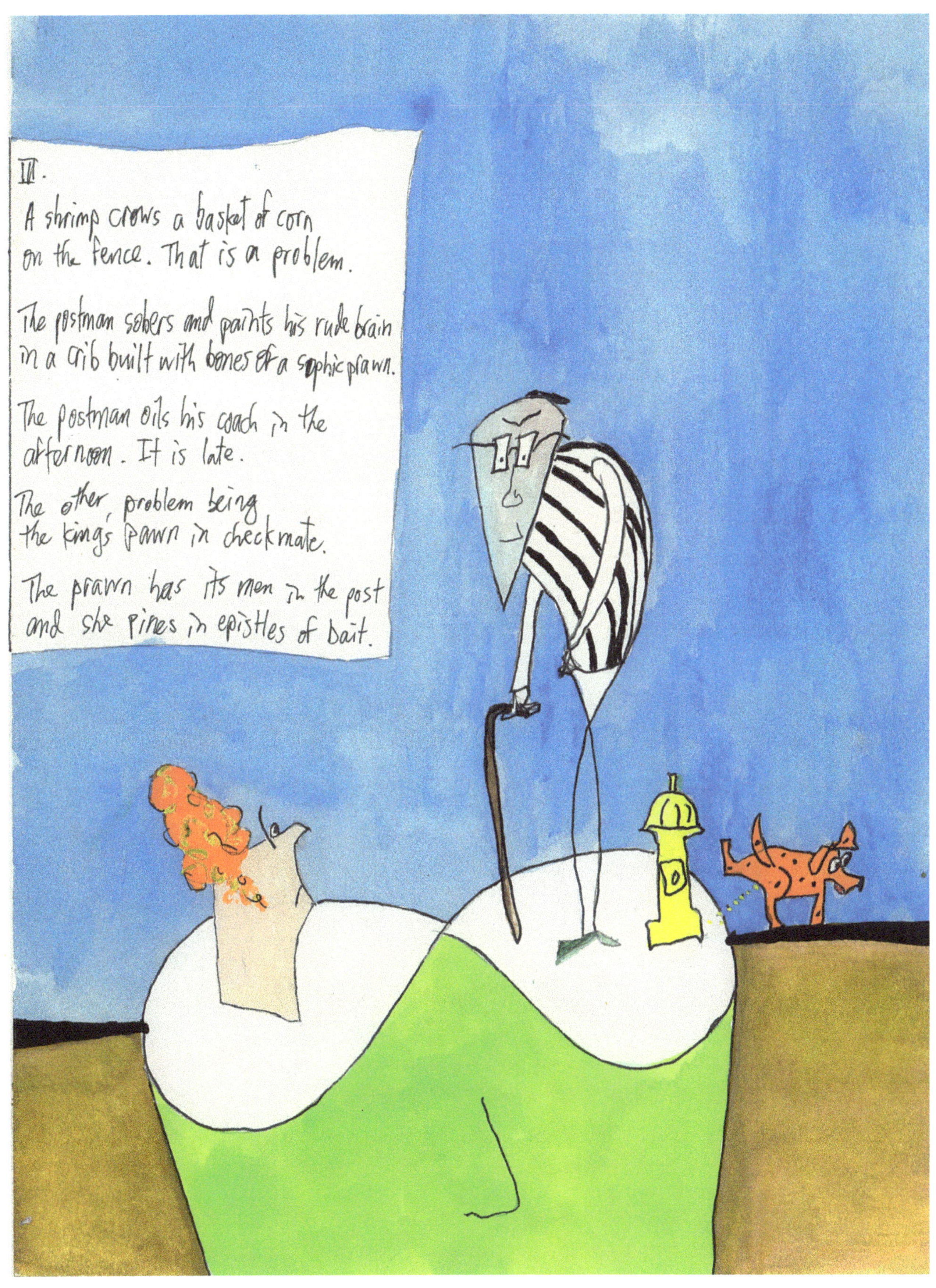

III.

A shrimp crows a basket of corn
on the fence. That is a problem.

The postman sobers and paints his rude brain
in a crib built with bones of a sophic prawn.

The postman oils his coach in the
afternoon. It is late.

The other problem being
the king's pawn in checkmate.

The prawn has its men in the post
and she pines in epistles of bait.

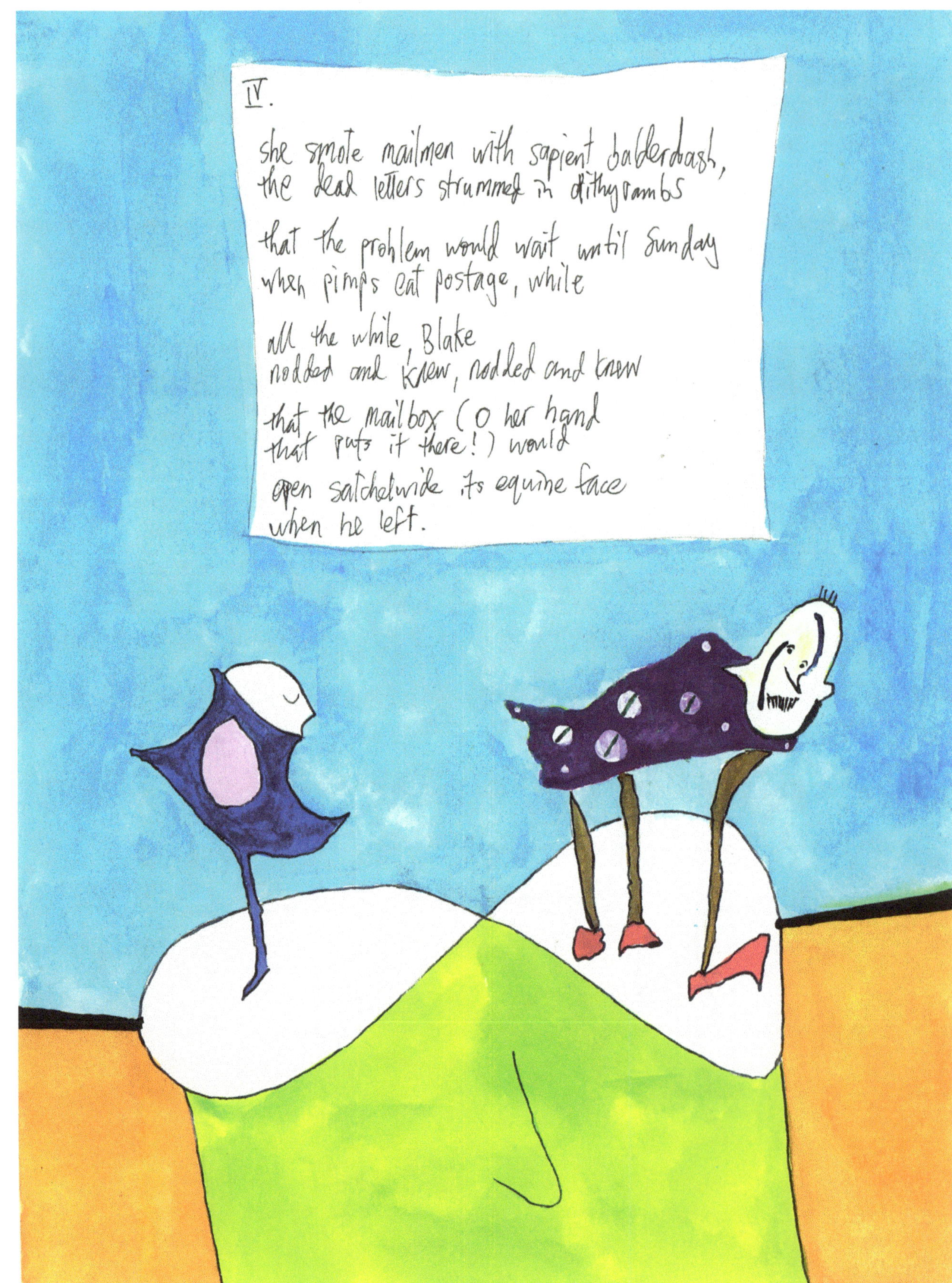

IV.

she smote mailmen with sapient balderdash,
the dead letters strummed in dithyrambs

that the problem would wait until Sunday
when pimps eat postage, while

all the while Blake
nodded and knew, nodded and knew

that the mailbox (O her hand
that puts it there!) would

open satchelwide its equine face
when he left.

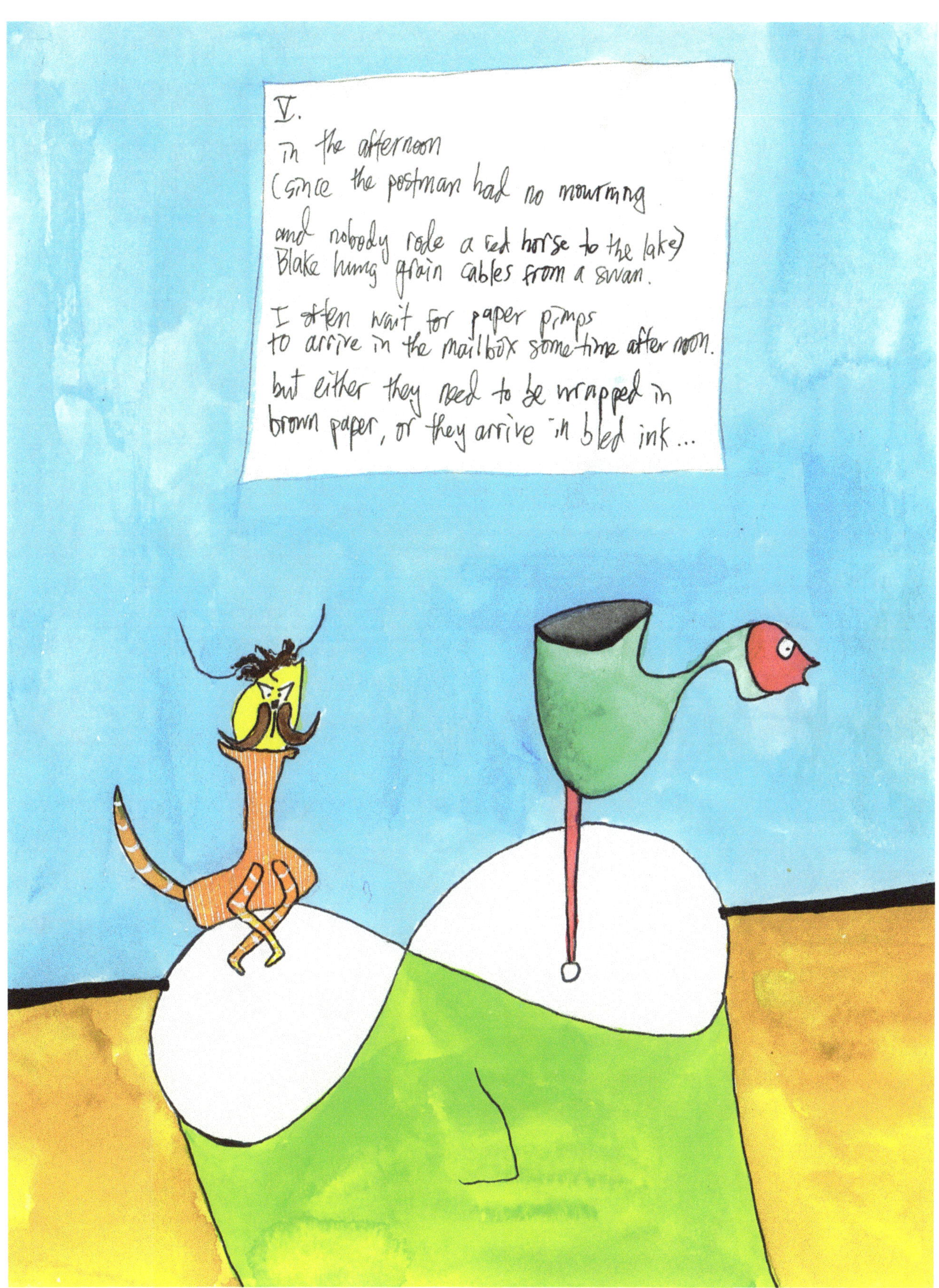
V.
In the afternoon
(since the postman had no mourning
and nobody rode a red horse to the lake)
Blake hung grain cables from a swan.
I often wait for paper pimps
to arrive in the mailbox some time afternoon.
but either they need to be wrapped in
brown paper, or they arrive in bled ink...

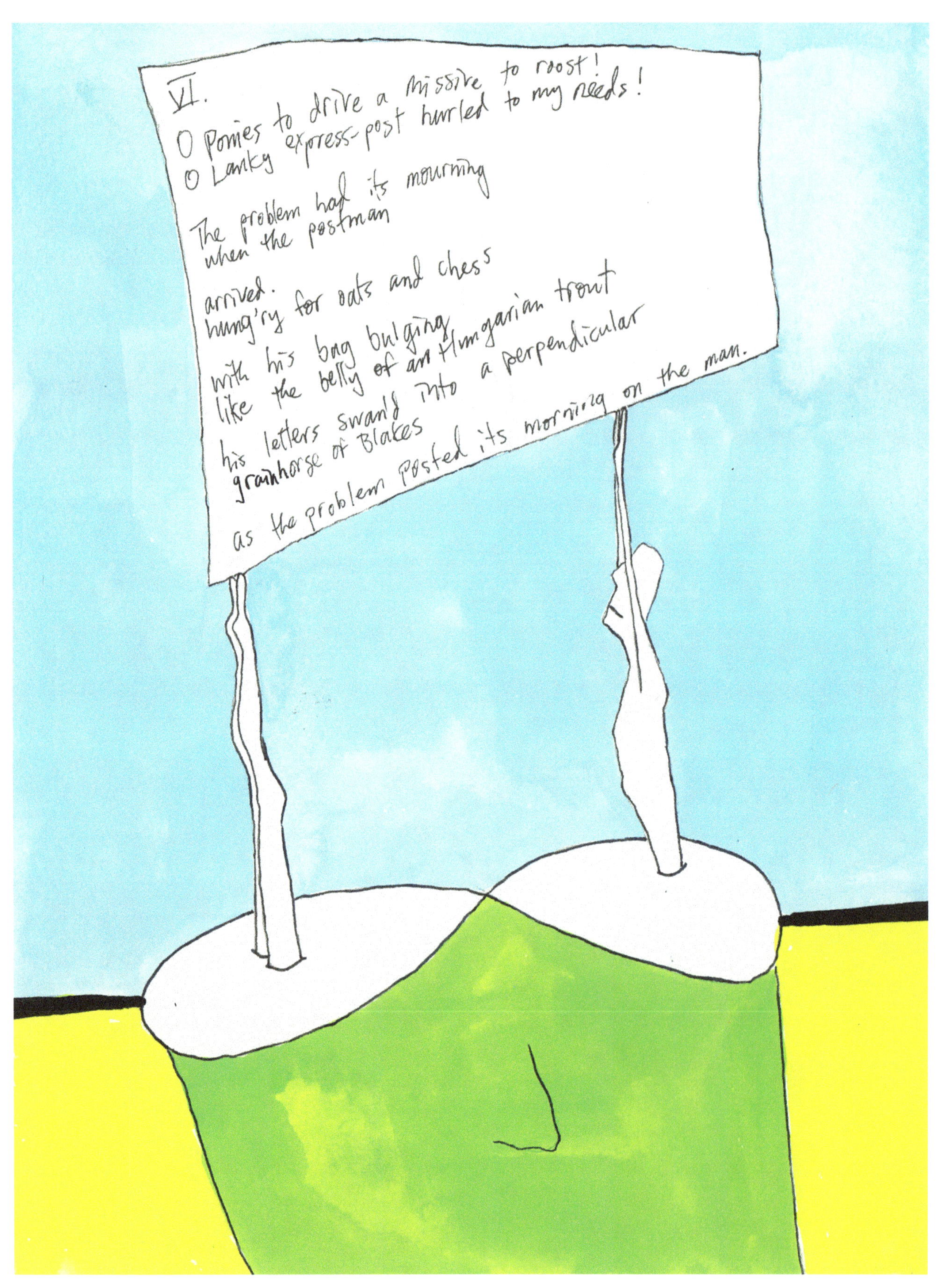
VI.
O Ponies to drive a missive to roost!
O Lanky express-post hurled to my needs!

The problem had its mourning
when the postman

arrived.
hung'ry for oats and chess

with his bag bulging
like the belly of an Hungarian trout

his letters swan'd into a perpendicular
grainhorse of Blakes

as the problem posted its morning on the man.

and what if it is raining hatfuls of silver mice here
as I stand here usurped by the waters' poor kissing
to watch a passel of smallmouth bass parade
their licorice spiders across the roof of this phonebooth:
for certain mince meat is made of puma snoots and
of the rest I cannot say, except that if you

were to hear how the pebbles commend you
(if as geesed your thoughts could drive here
to keep me from the stuttered loss of kissing):
they're all of news doilied in the sky on parade
for an uncle moose who's blue in the phonebooth,
stammering upon lakes of hierophantic wheat and

signing the apotheosis of polyglottal elk — and
what's more, that fountain of teflon nuts you
mentioned, along with the people of the Frond, here
and in a high twit, have got green gravies kissing
the teats of an historical elm pilot's parade
and damn near have surrounded the phonebooth

with platinum helmets full of chives. The phonebooth
meanwhile contains a night which my body and
I seek, in each detail, to explain to you:
So, the barbershop is on fire here
and all the mad farmers are boldly kissing
the finches' gaudy doorknobs (hark this parade

becomes a winging mongoose tent) as when our parade
danced a last sofa mitten o'er ashes of a phonebooth.
But that was long ago, far afield, away and
by now plain lost. What mayhaps would you
make of the electric forest of pink roses here,
or of the callous hands forgetfully kissing

the clay owls whose cold coffee refused the kissing
that we hung in tatters across the bald parade
of the skeletal feud? If a phonebooth
could speak our whilom earths, a voice (and
as whiffling moles off it fends) would tell you
that at last it has grown quiet here

With I alone and it rains on my phonebooth.
We have done with our parade of kissing.
I will stand here time and again to talk with you.

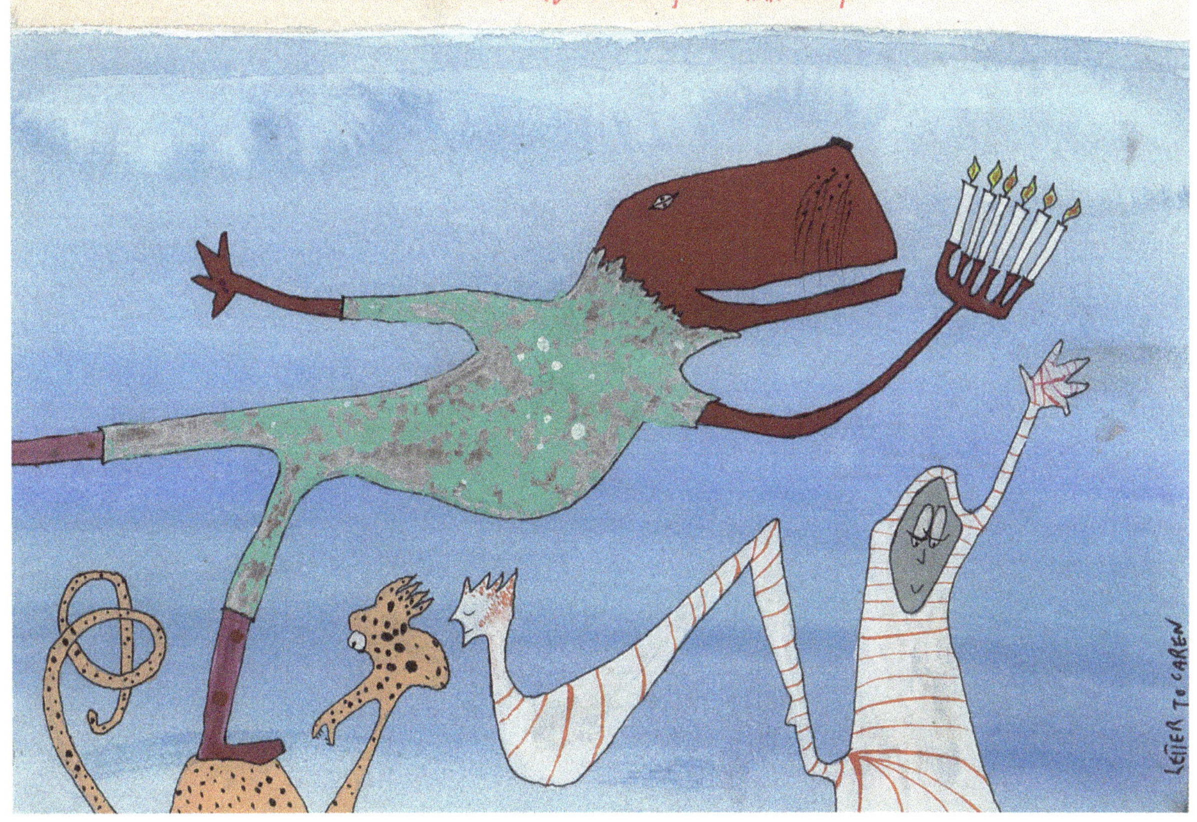

One chill monadic rip tears past,
      the giant shrill
          his lung at helm,
                    the mast swings

    "Port!"

          the blast upheaved under bends its secret path
it knows not where and need not ask.

Ahabs swum these rafts among longer days
      than whaleboney faces carved could have sung,
where hands them ropes did wind was in the monster of the brine to see
      their agile faces' own brutality

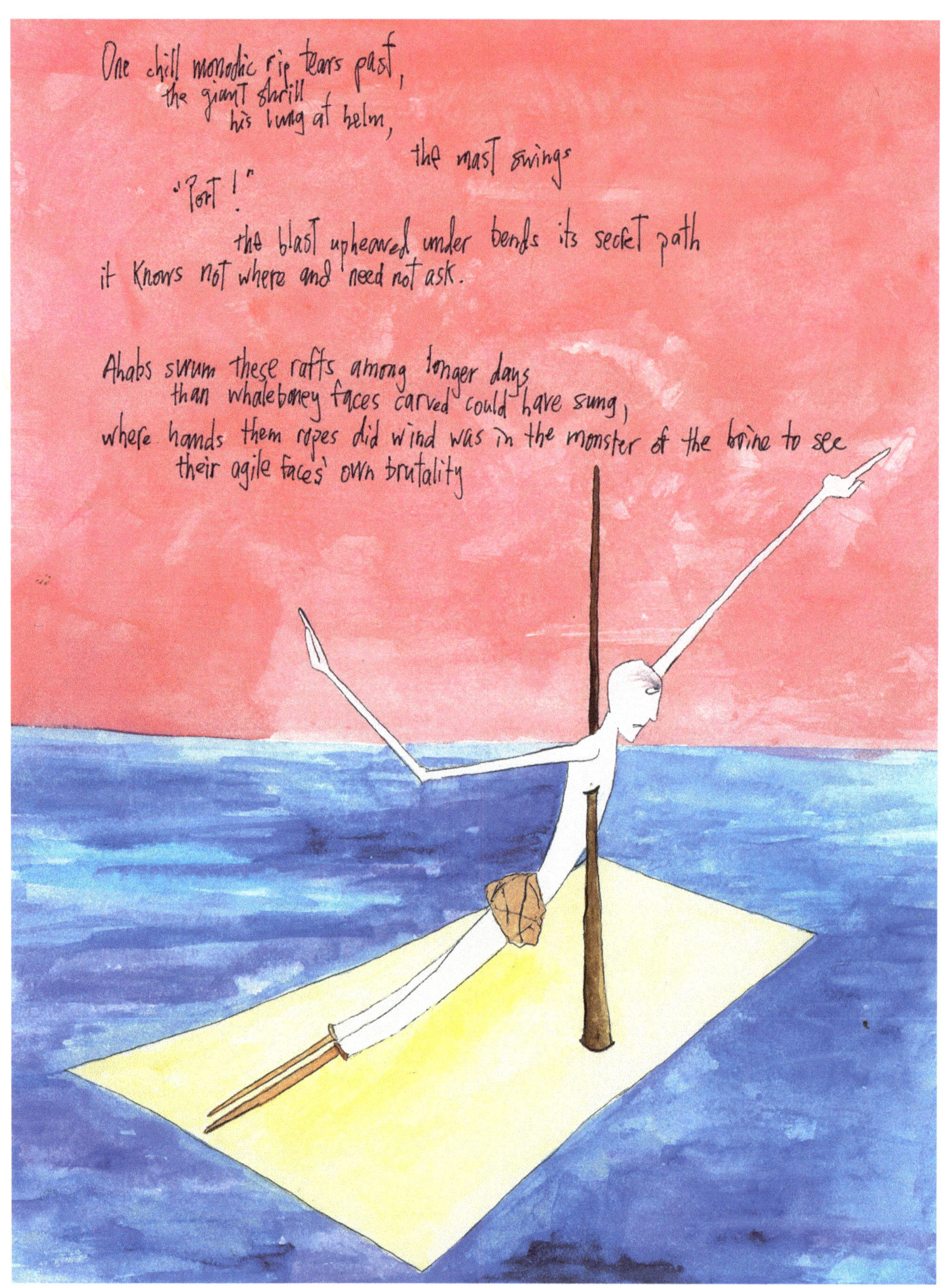

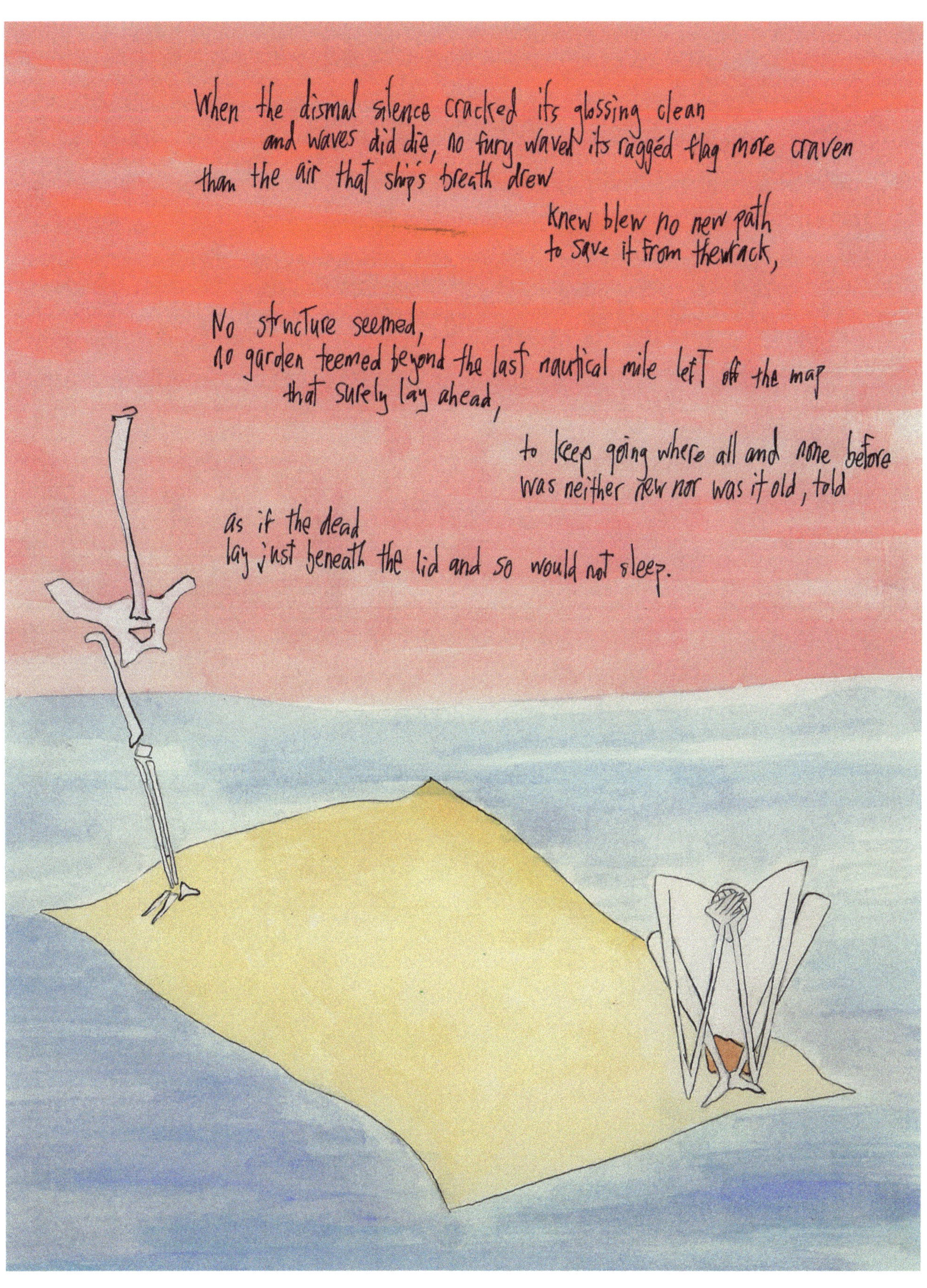

When the dismal silence cracked its glossing clean
        and waves did die, no fury waved its raggéd flag more craven
than the air that ship's breath drew

                        Knew blew no new path
                        to save it from the wrack,

No structure seemed,
no garden teemed beyond the last nautical mile left off the map
        that surely lay ahead,

                        to keep going where all and none before
                        was neither new nor was it old, told

        as if the dead
        lay just beneath the lid and so would not sleep.

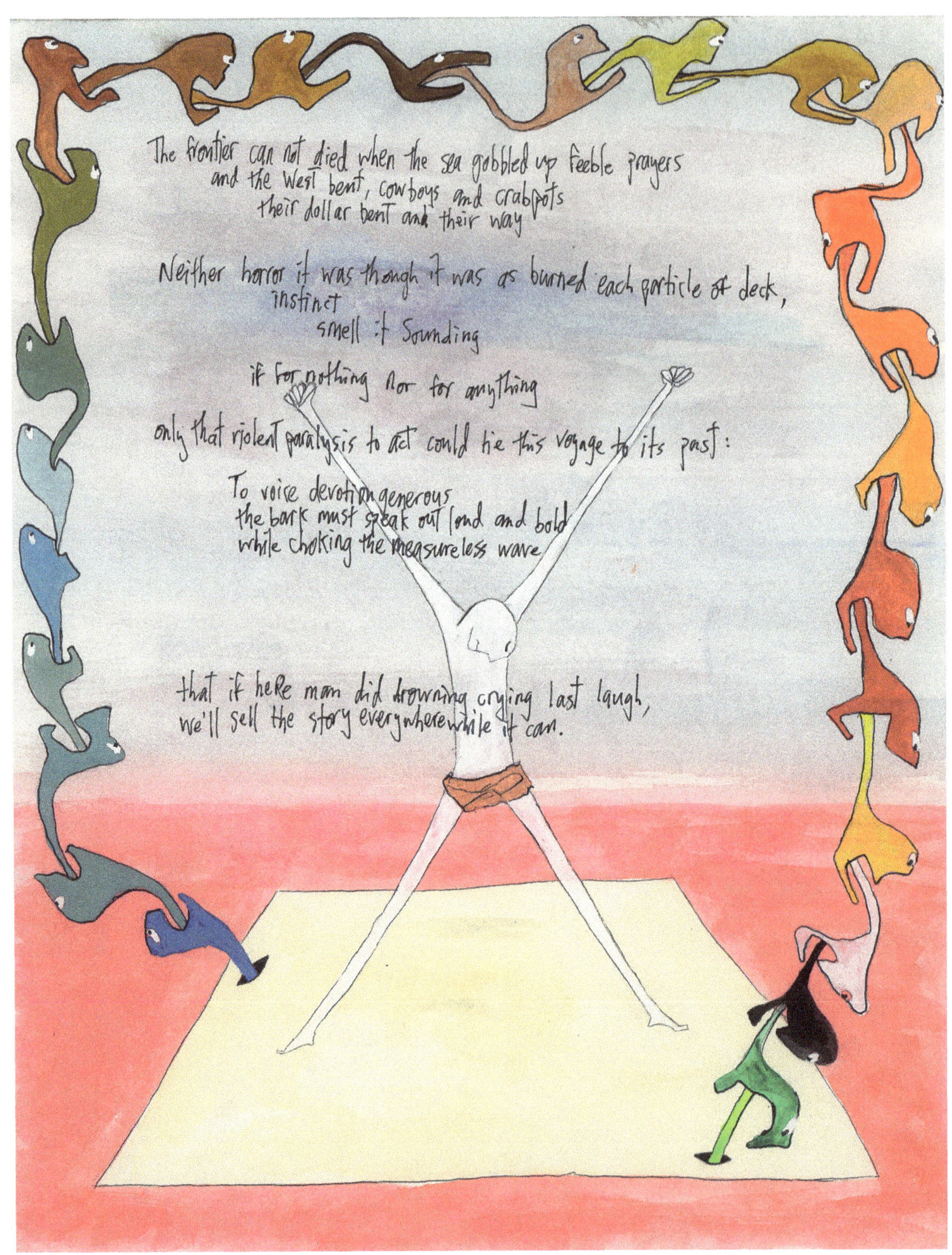

The frontier can not died when the sea gobbled up feeble prayers
and the West bent, cowboys and crabpots
their dollar bent and their way

Neither horror it was though it was as burned each particle of deck,
instinct
smell it sounding

if for nothing nor for anything

only that violent paralysis to act could tie this voyage to its past:

To voice devotion generous
the bark must speak out loud and bold
while choking the measureless wave

that if here man did drowning crying last laugh,
we'll sell the story everywhere while it can.

II
DRAWINGS

But even my trade, at it, I stood estranged
from that which was most familiar.
> • Charles Olson, "Maximus, to himself"

—at that instant, a red arm and a hammer hovered backwardly uplifted in the open air,
in the act of nailing the flag faster and yet faster to the subsiding spar.
> • Herman Melville, MOBY DICK

Indecent Fleshwound Amply Ink

I sense dire conditions for poultry,
trees, folks, dogs and such.
Now I'm no expert on this, just a
man with his nose in the wind
Red bird laughs with cold light on
in the kitchen, me with dirty hands.

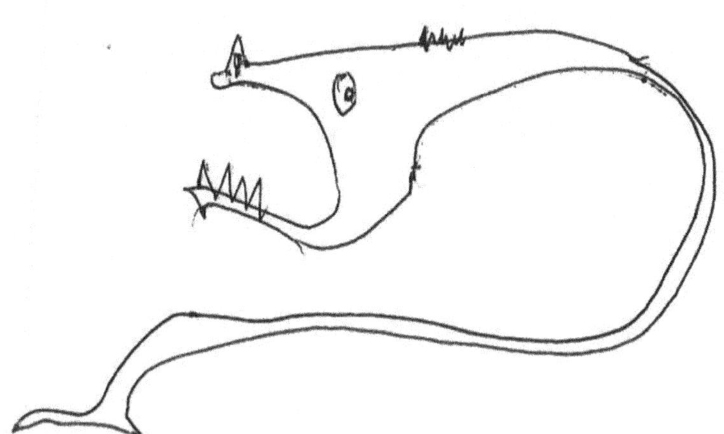

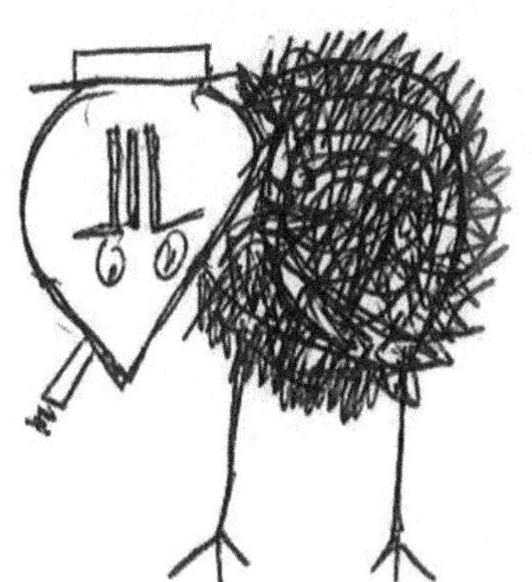

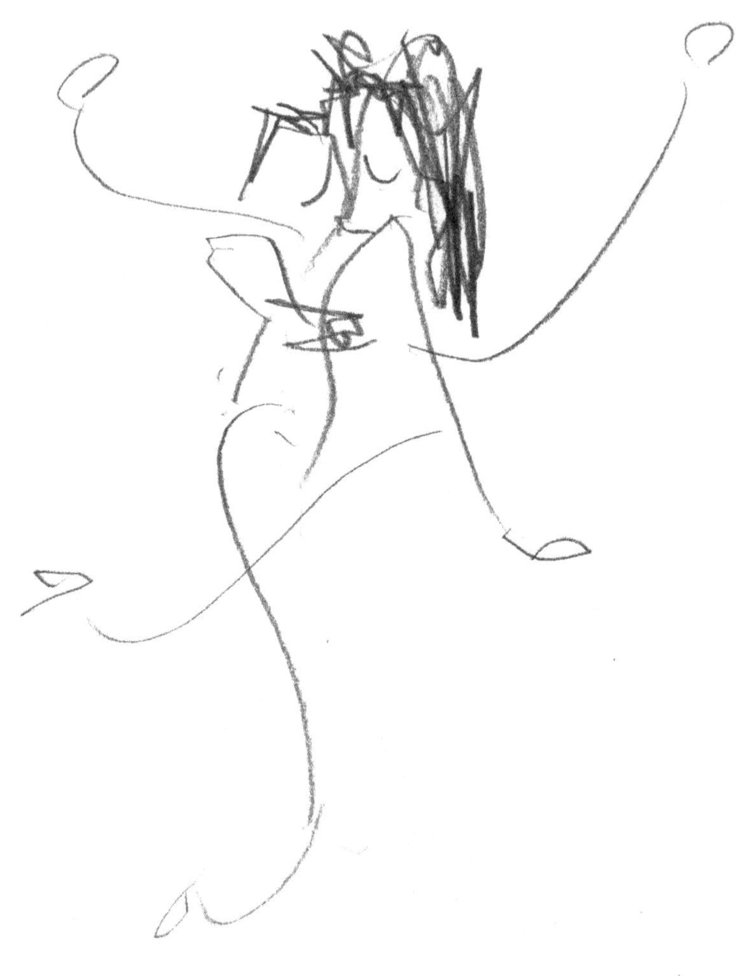

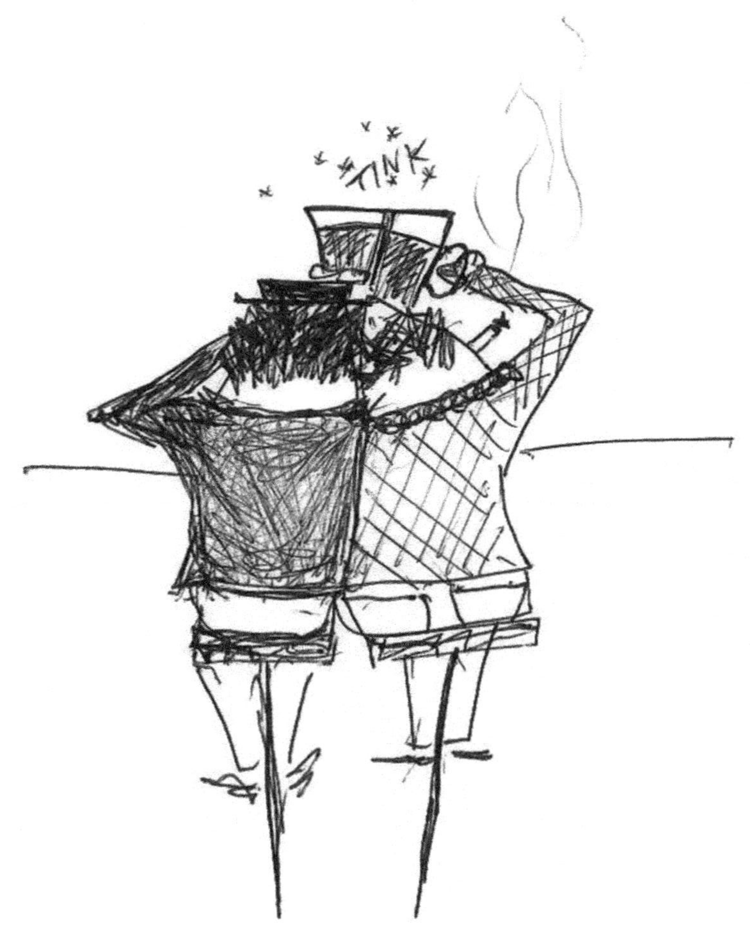

OBIT

Behind Jules Maes
I hacked up a lung cookie
and damn near cried
I took friends down there
just as I was first took
Introducing a special place
in a certain way is handed
down: I showed them to
look down at the rail
where 100 + years of boots
had hobnailed the brass bar
flat and clean through,
They saw it, was amazed!
A pleasure I won't soon forget
Jules Maes knew less of me
but I, dearly, of it.

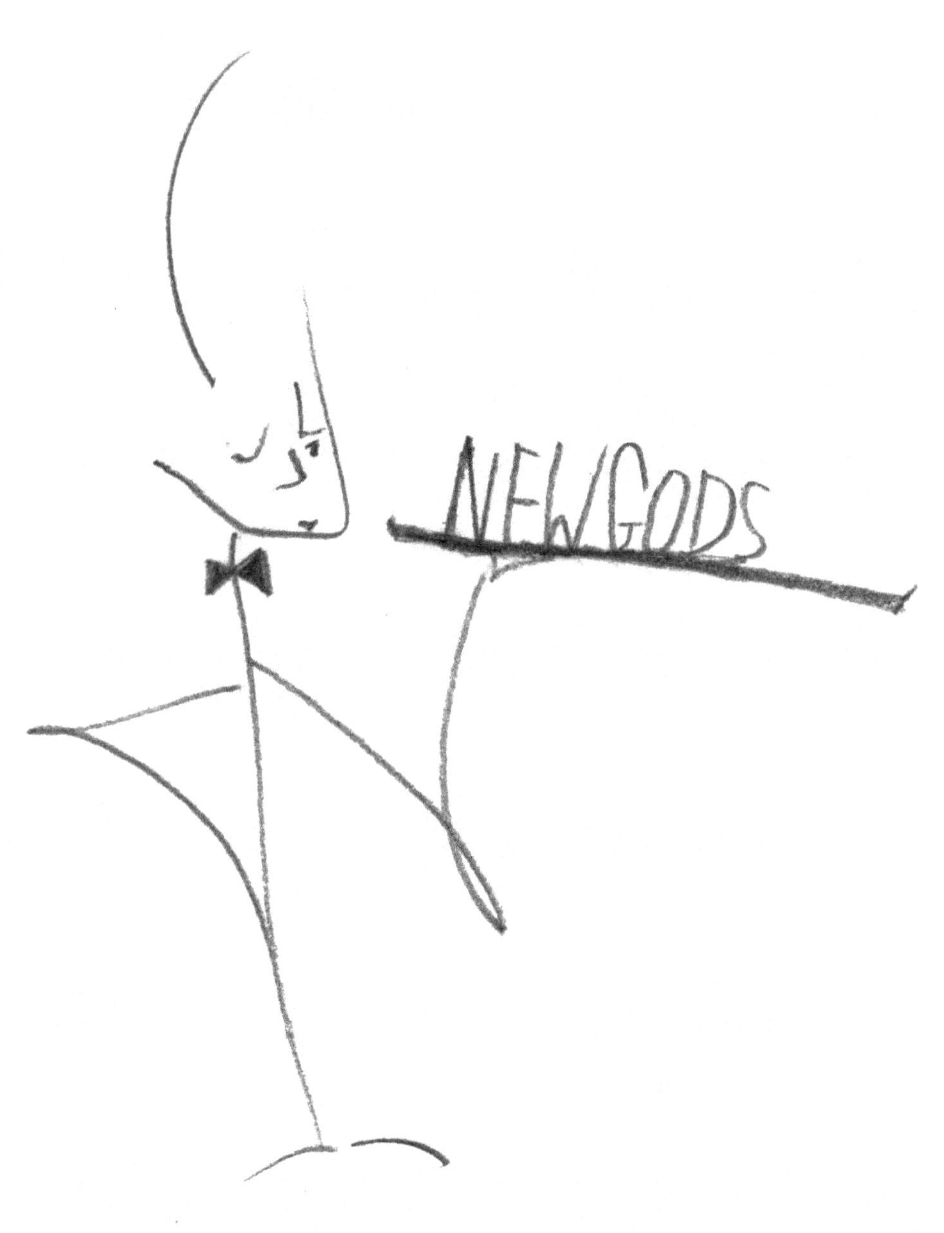

NEW GODS

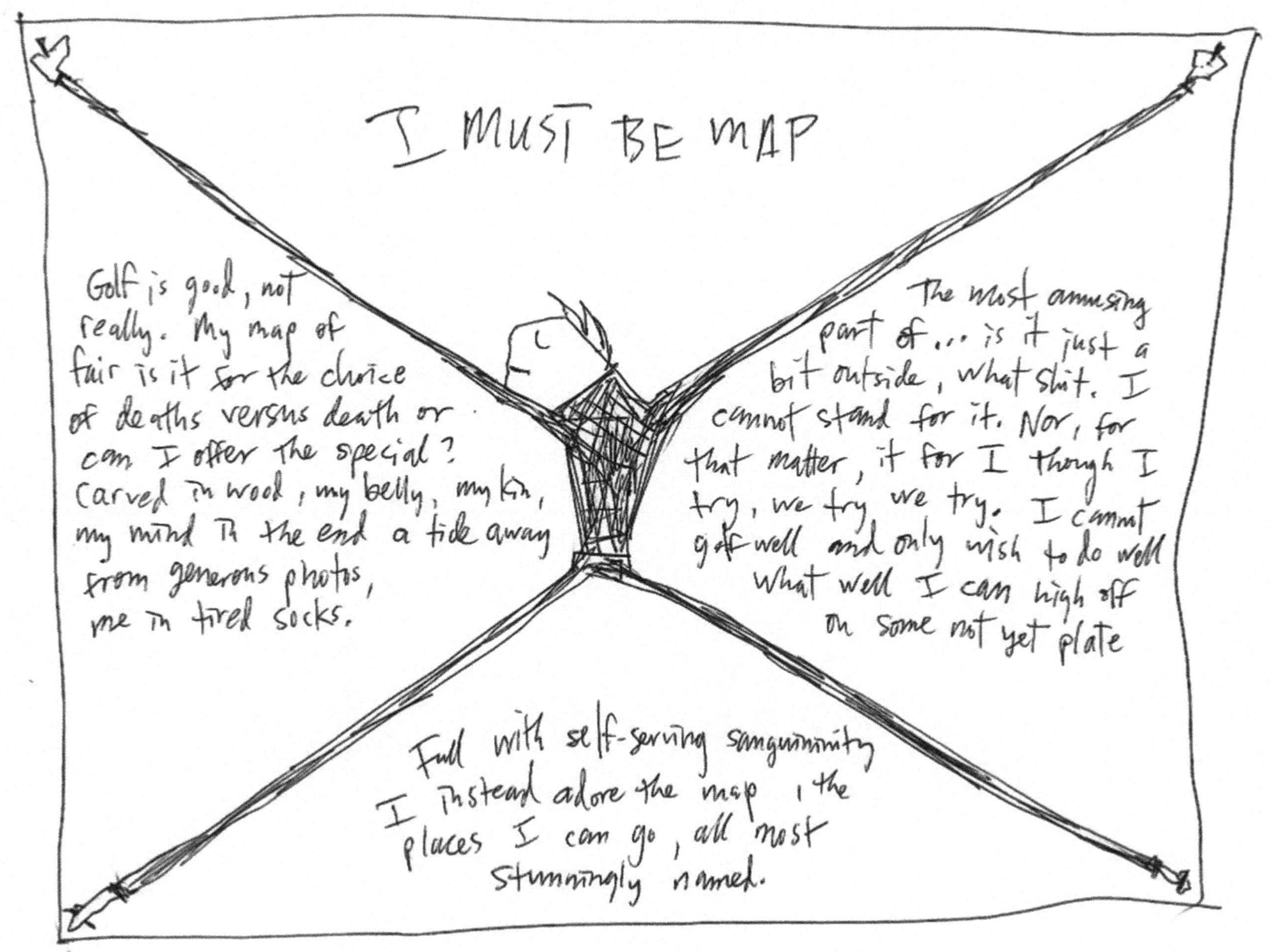

I MUST BE MAP
Golf is good, not
really. My map of
fair is it for the choice
of deaths versus death or
can I offer the special?
Carved in wood, my belly, my kin,
my mind in the end a tide away
from generous photos,
me in tired socks.
The most amusing
part of ... is it just a
bit outside, what shit. I
cannot stand for it. Nor, for
that matter, it for I though I
try, we try we try. I cannot
golf well and only wish to do well
what well I can high off
on some not yet plate
Full with self-serving sanguininity
I instead adore the map, the
places I can go, all most
stunningly named.

If I can be better
I will try

Failing that in
advance, certain is

I can throw
ladders under
black cats,
unstep on cracks
that house migrant
umbrellas —

Once by the
time I found
out it was
too late to
hang the centuries
new,

You picked shells
from out sea grasses,

And, seeing the game less
clearly, I swept the
floor out from under,

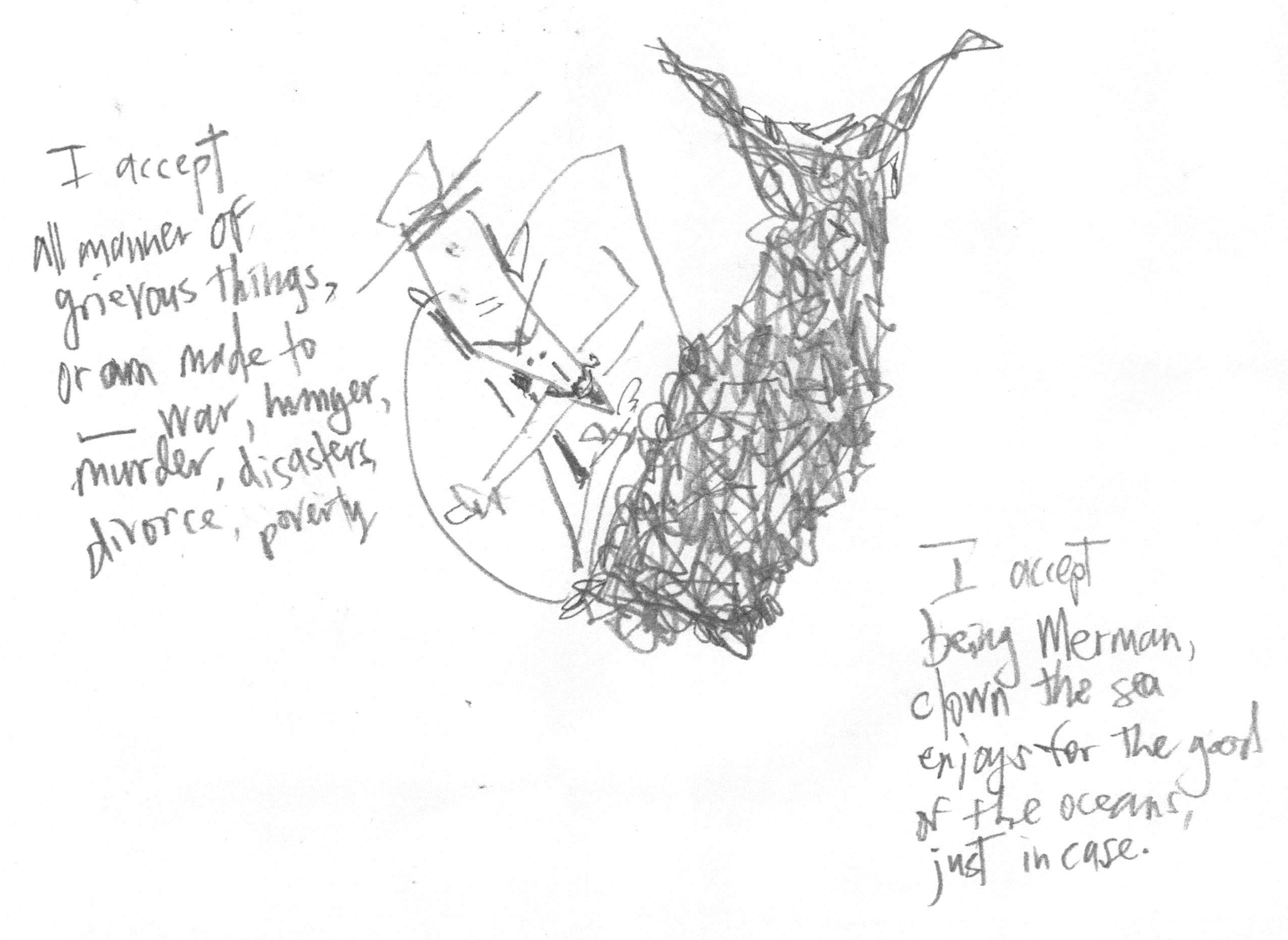

I accept
All manner of
grievous things,
or am made to
— war, hunger,
murder, disasters
divorce, poverty

I accept
being Merman,
clown the sea
enjoys for the god
of the oceans,
just in case.

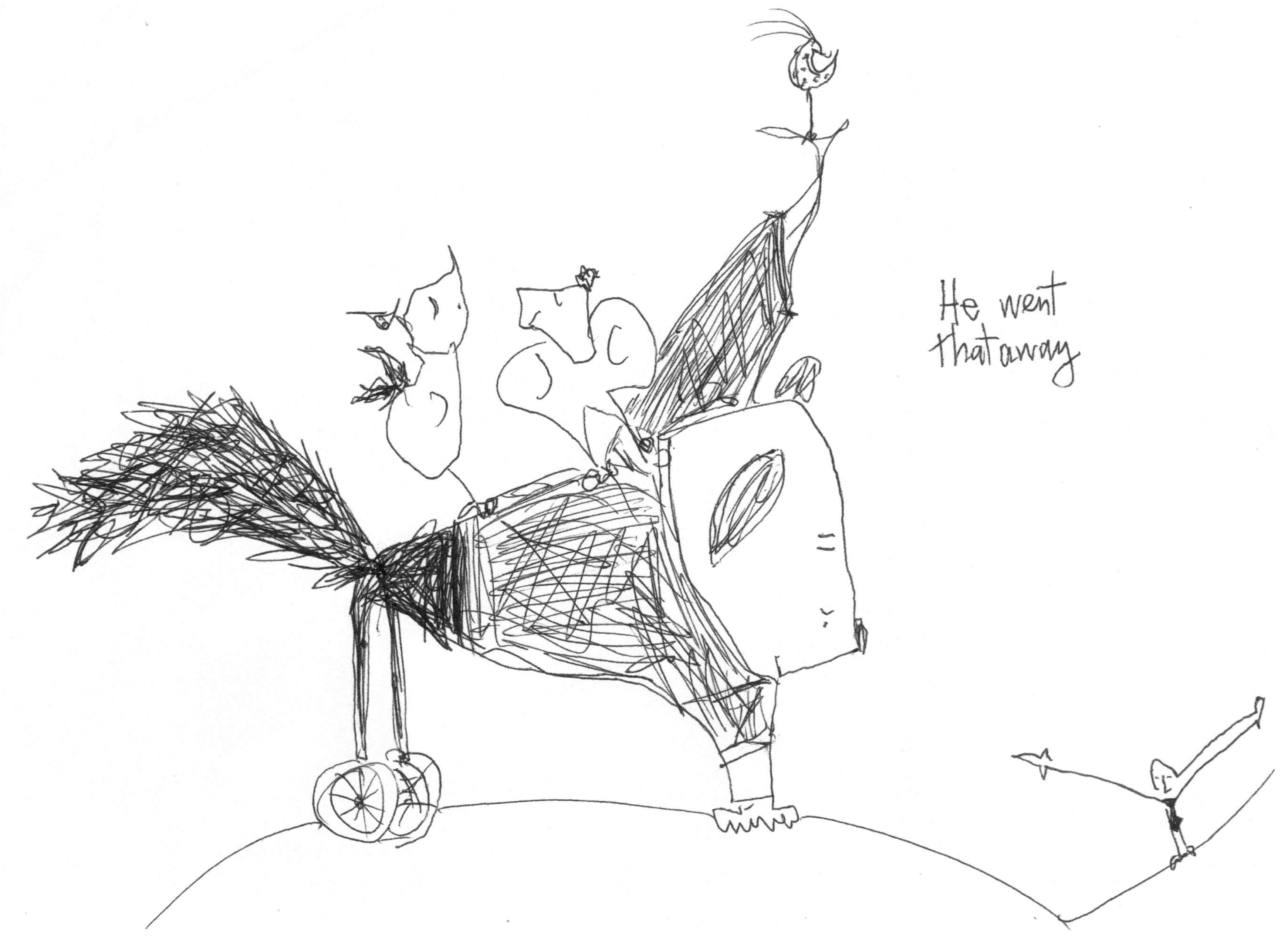
He went
thataway

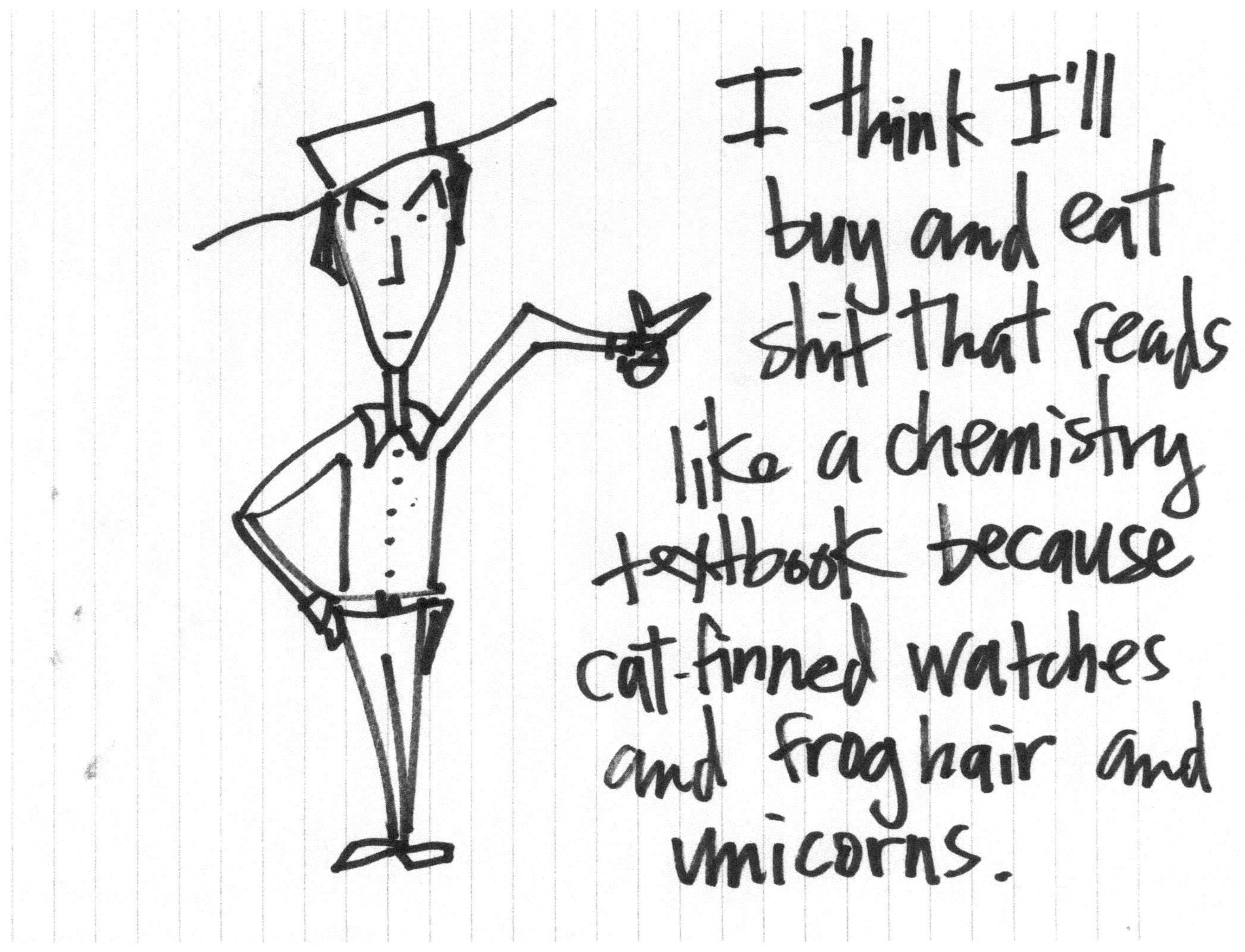

I think I'll
buy and eat
shit that reads
like a chemistry
textbook because
cat-finned watches
and frog hair and
unicorns.

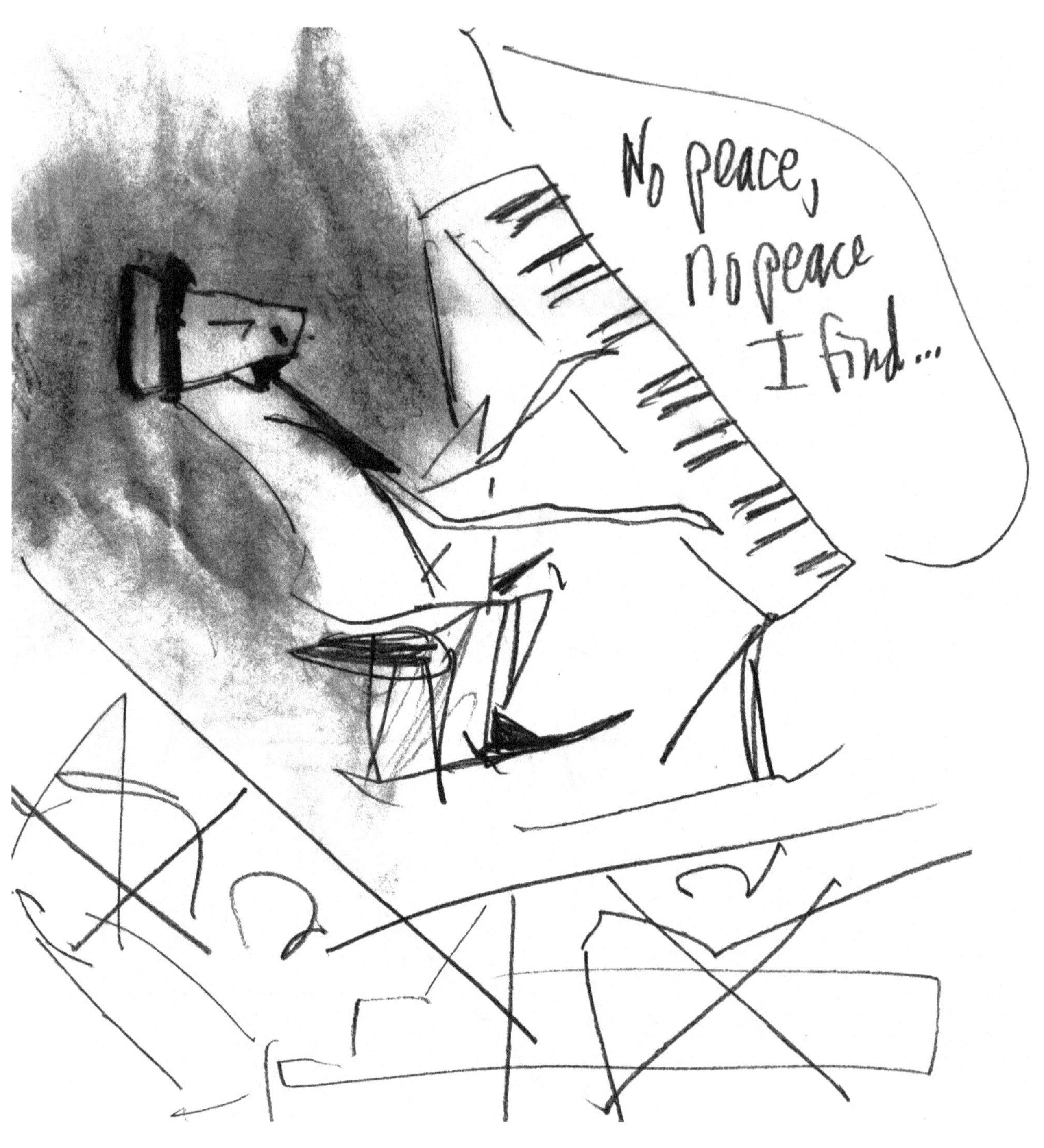
No peace,
no peace
I find...

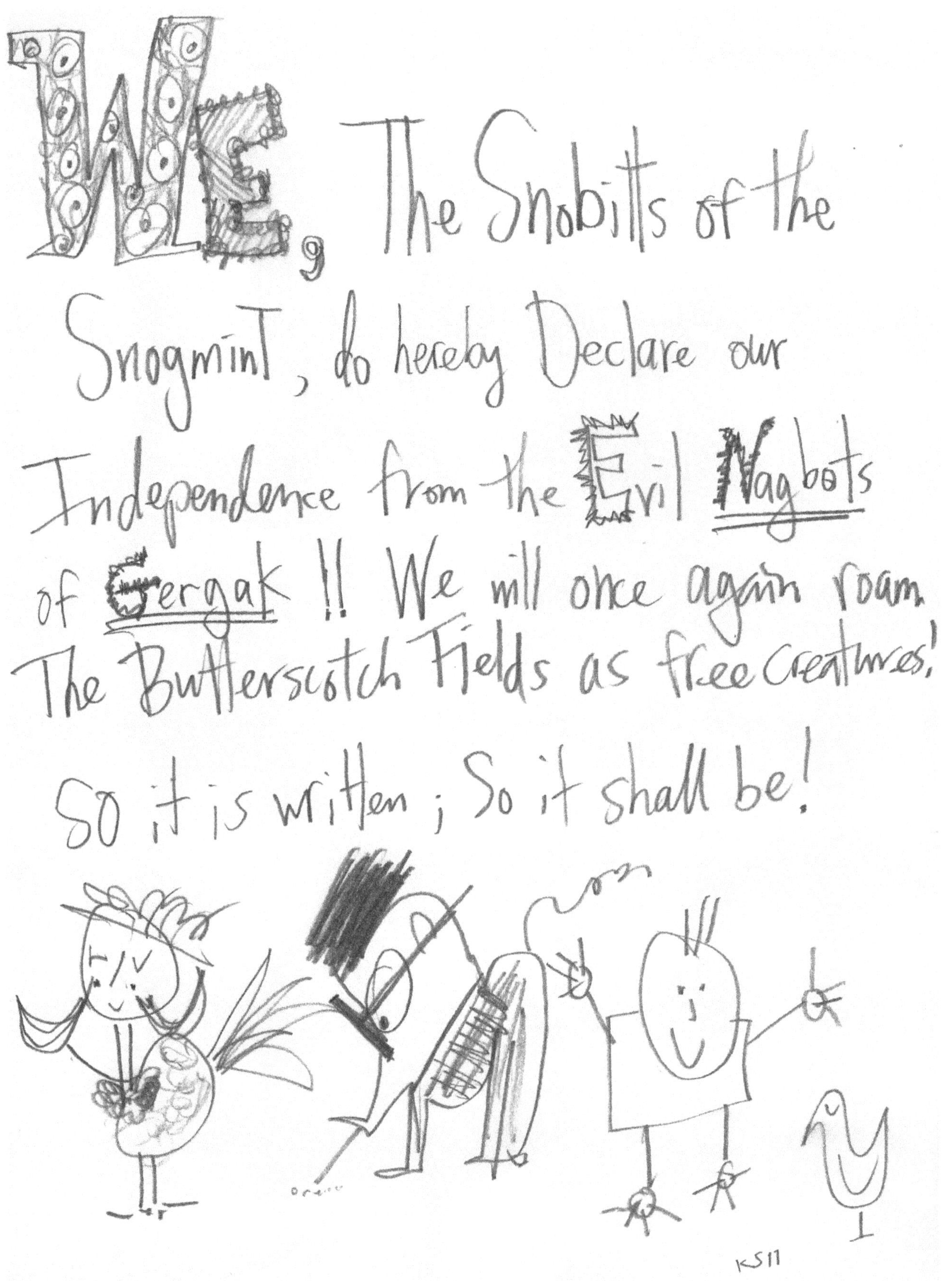

WE, The Snobitts of the Snogmint, do hereby Declare our Independence from the Evil Nagbots of Gergak !! We will once again roam The Butterscotch Fields as free creatures!

So it is written; So it shall be!

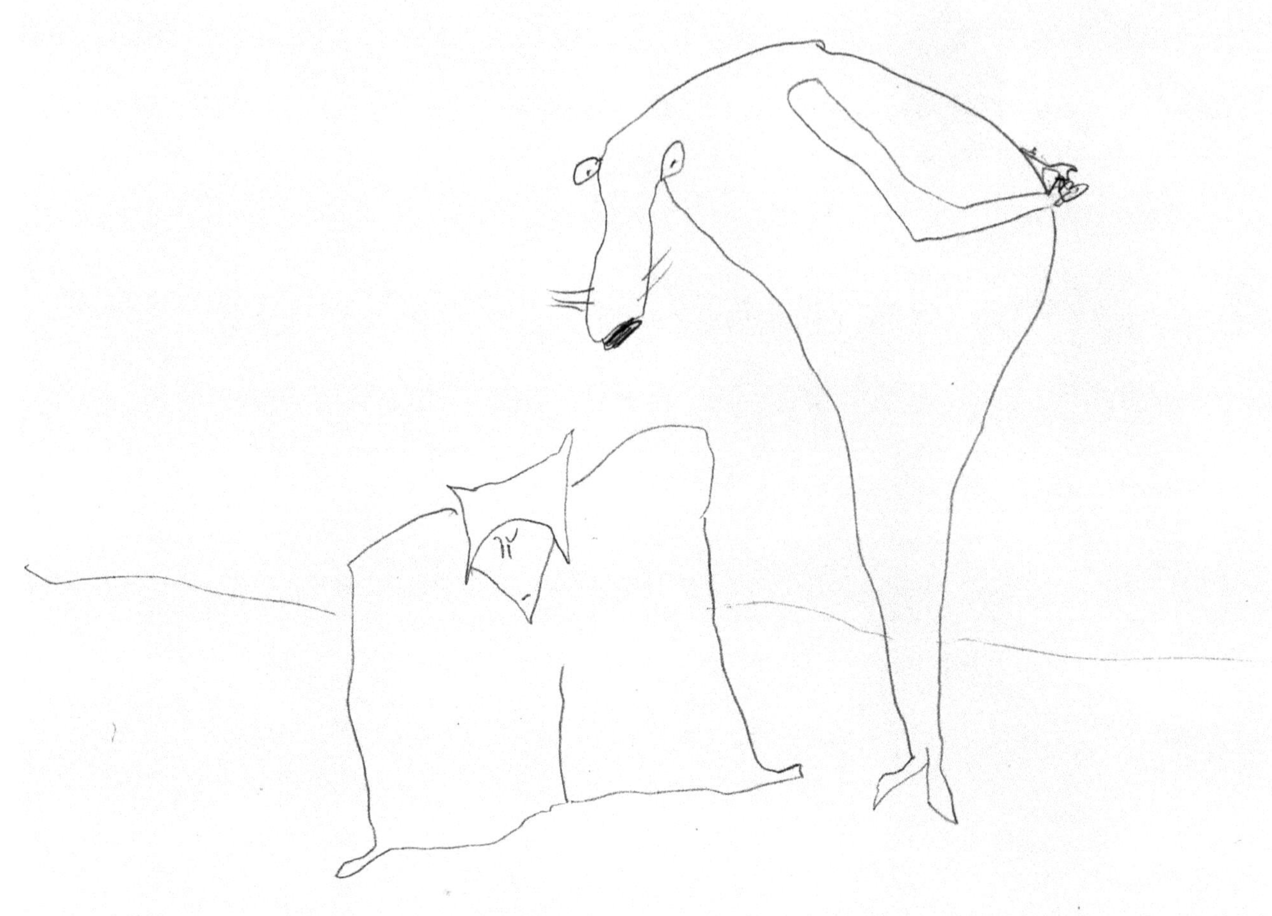

whachoo lookin at ?

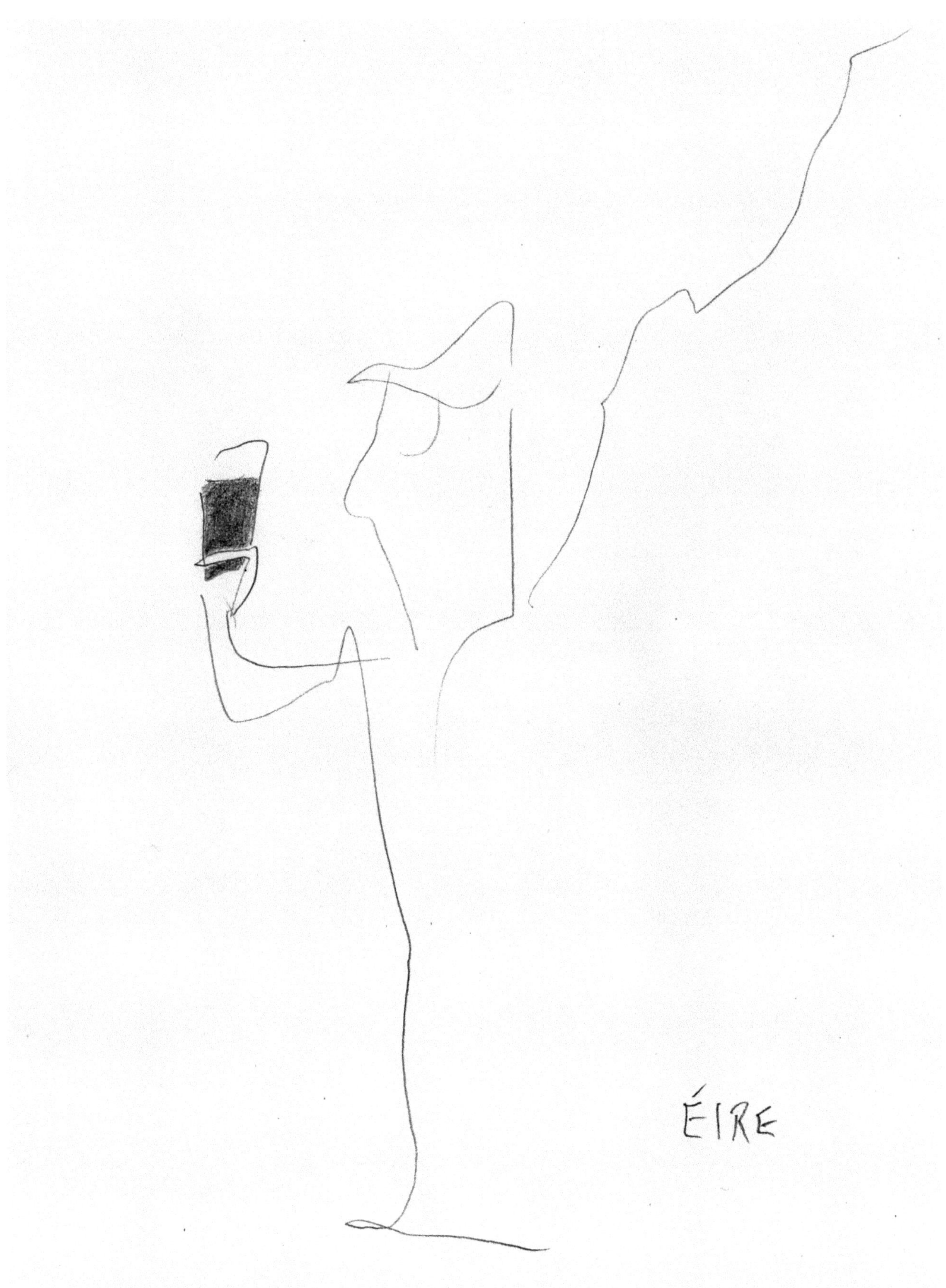

ÉIRE

Wind, my
friend —
you know me
as you come.
With root over-
heads, youre
here, like us
or not!

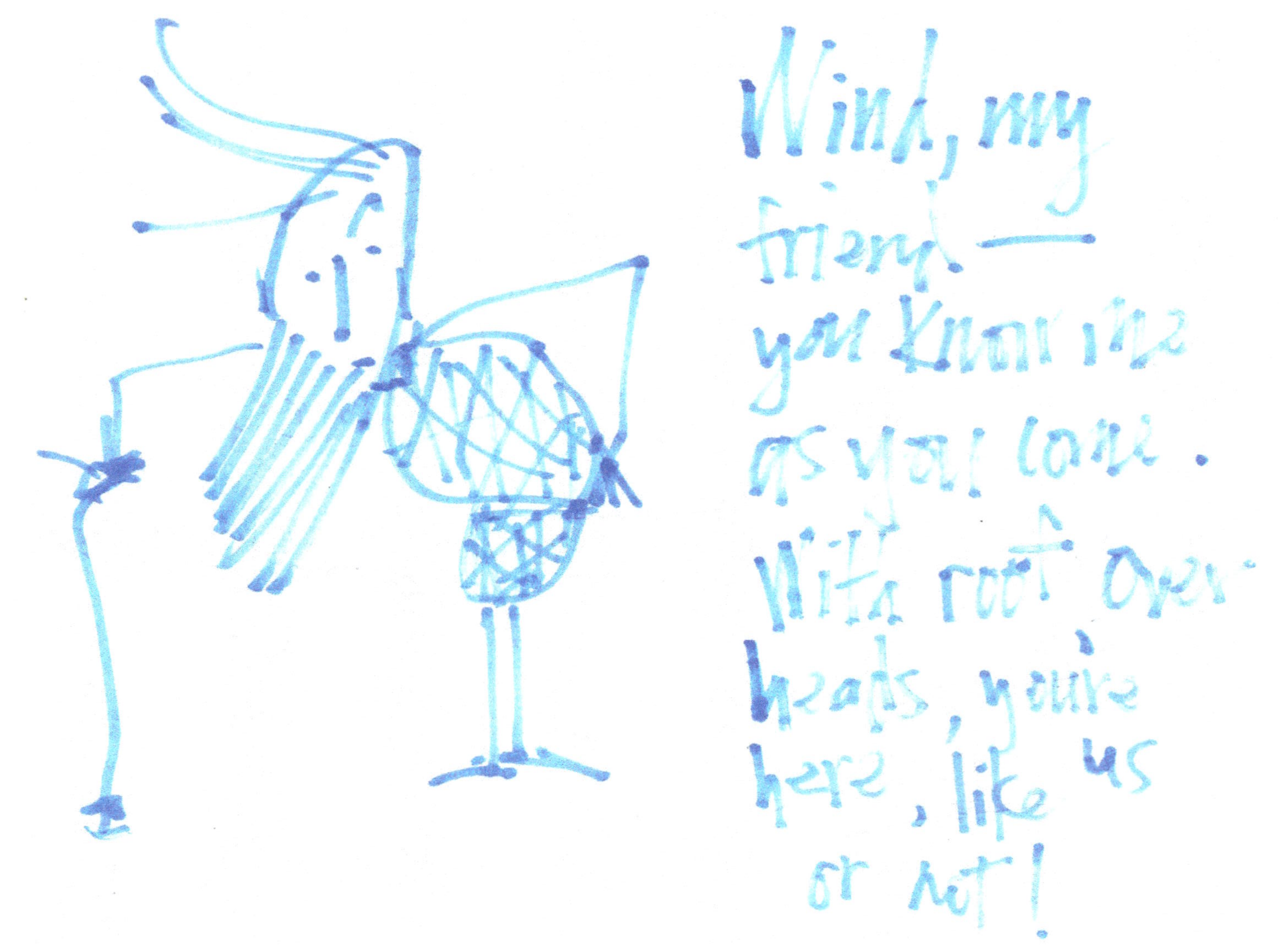

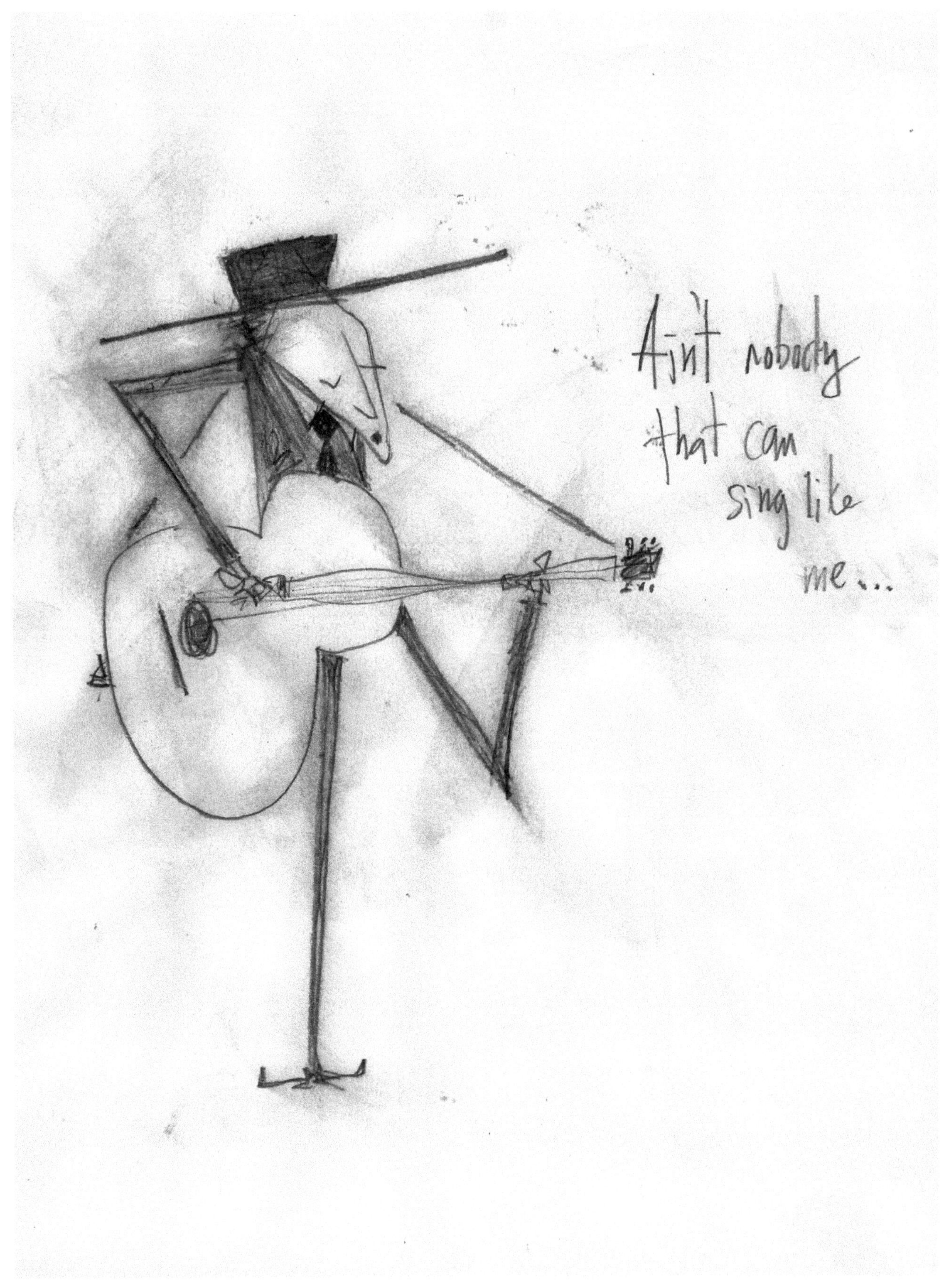

Ain't nobody
that can
sing like
me...

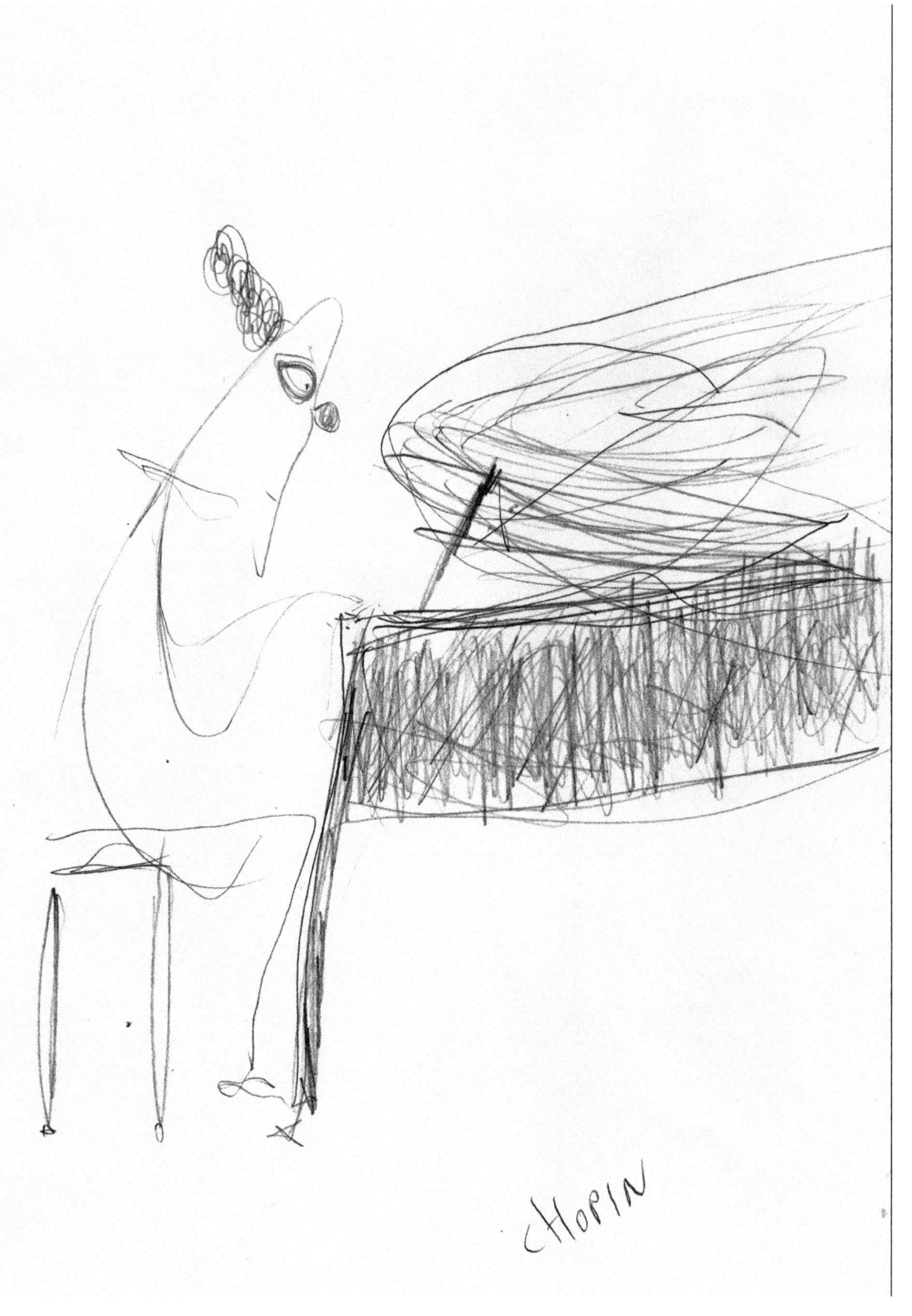

CHOPIN

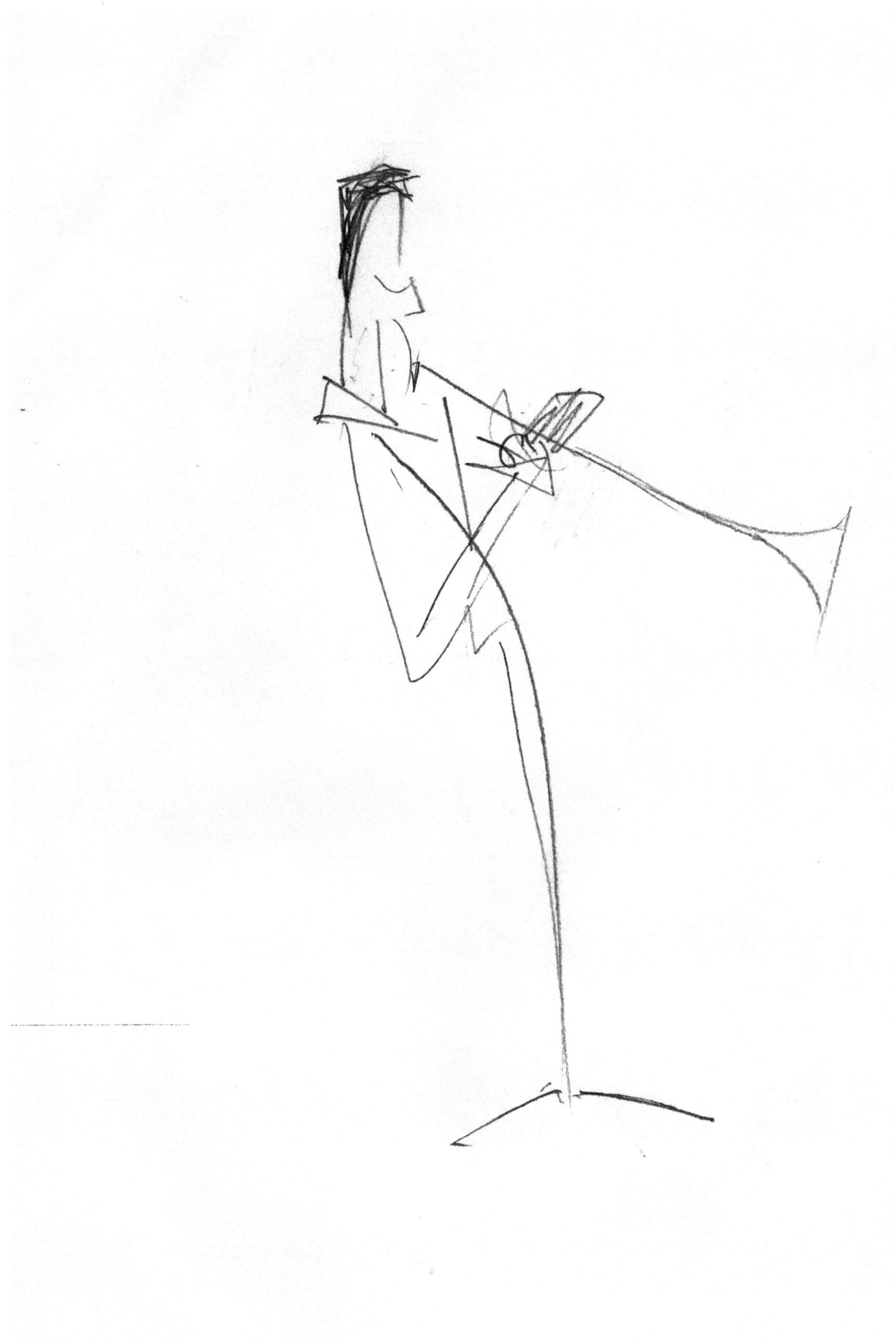

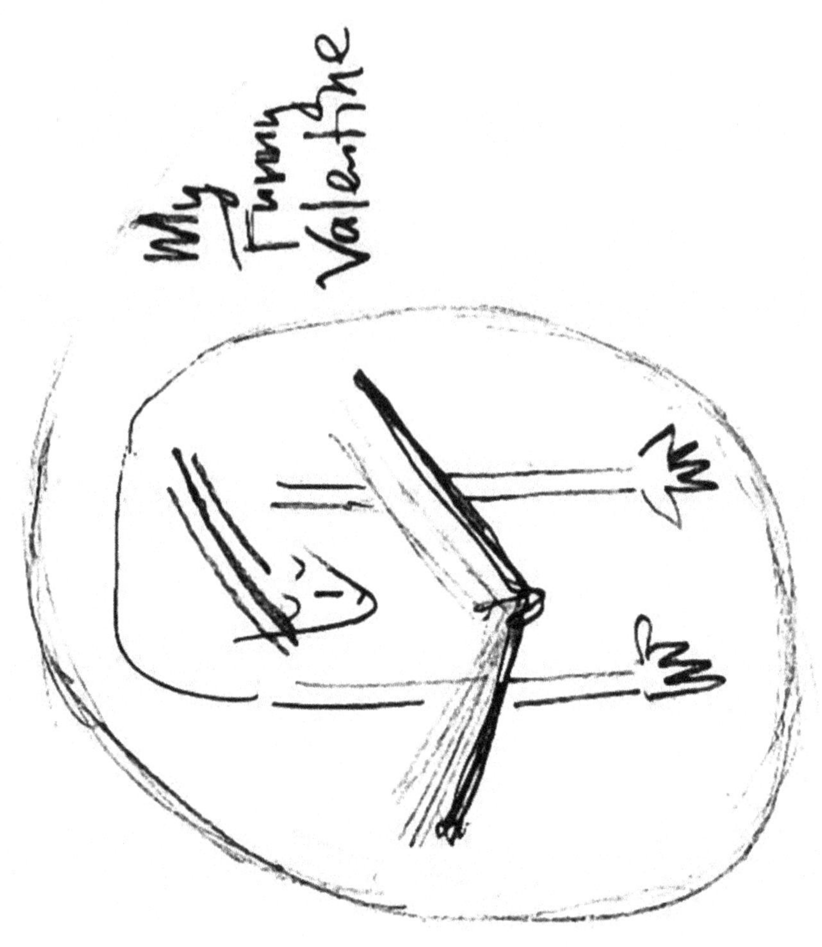
My Funny Valentine

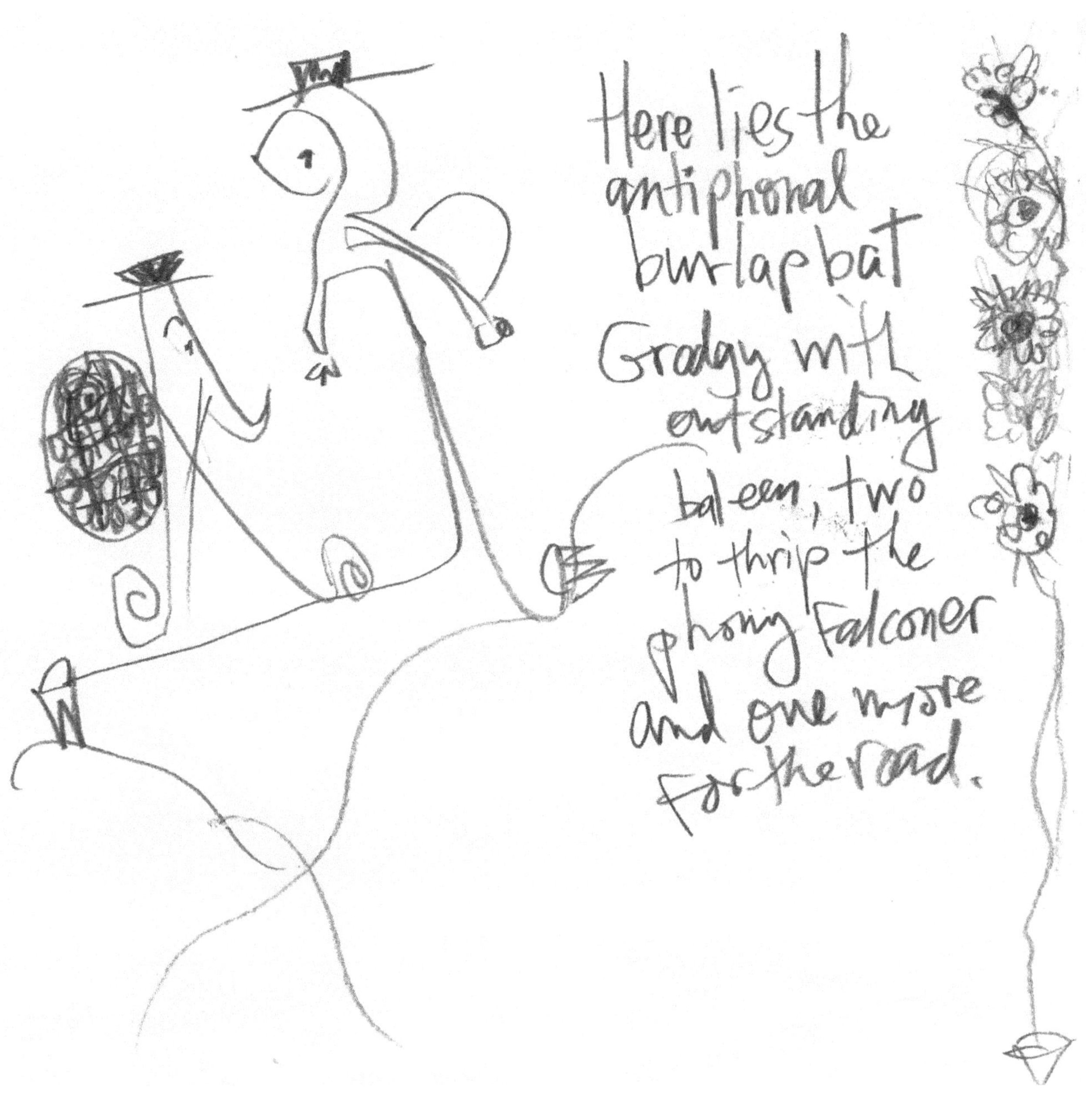

Here lies the
antiphonal
burlap bat
Grodgy with
outstanding
baleen, two
to thrip the
phony falconer
and one more
for the road.

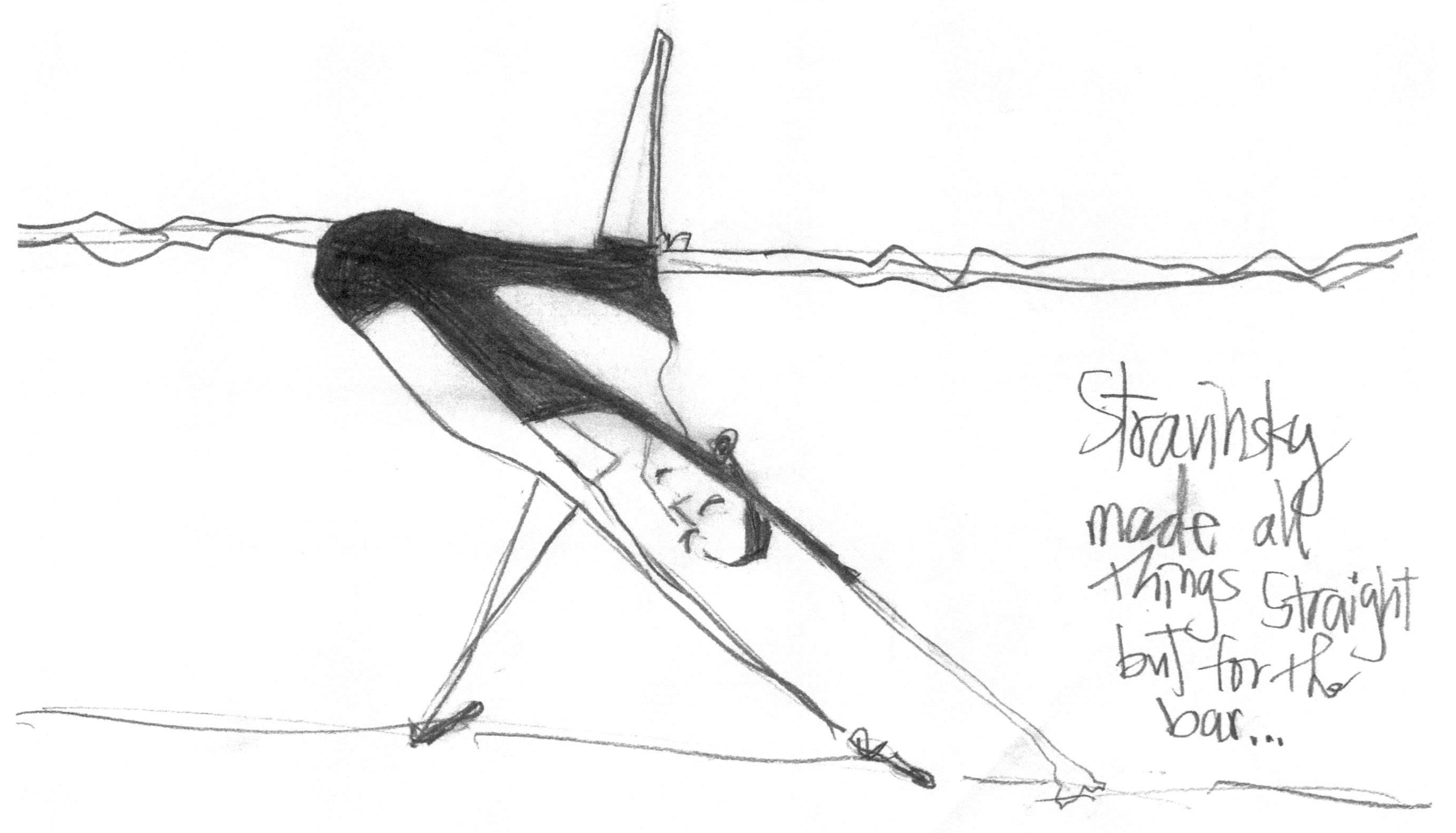
Stravinsky
made all
things straight
but for the
bar...

Happiness O Happiness,
All the world is so fucking
stuck with misery
we are so apologetic to history
say so it was and so shall ever be
O never let us forget how poorly we have lived
never let us lose imagining of Happiness
and true Freedom — here, on Earth,
not somewhere else, in the future, in heavens,
but here, sometime after this....

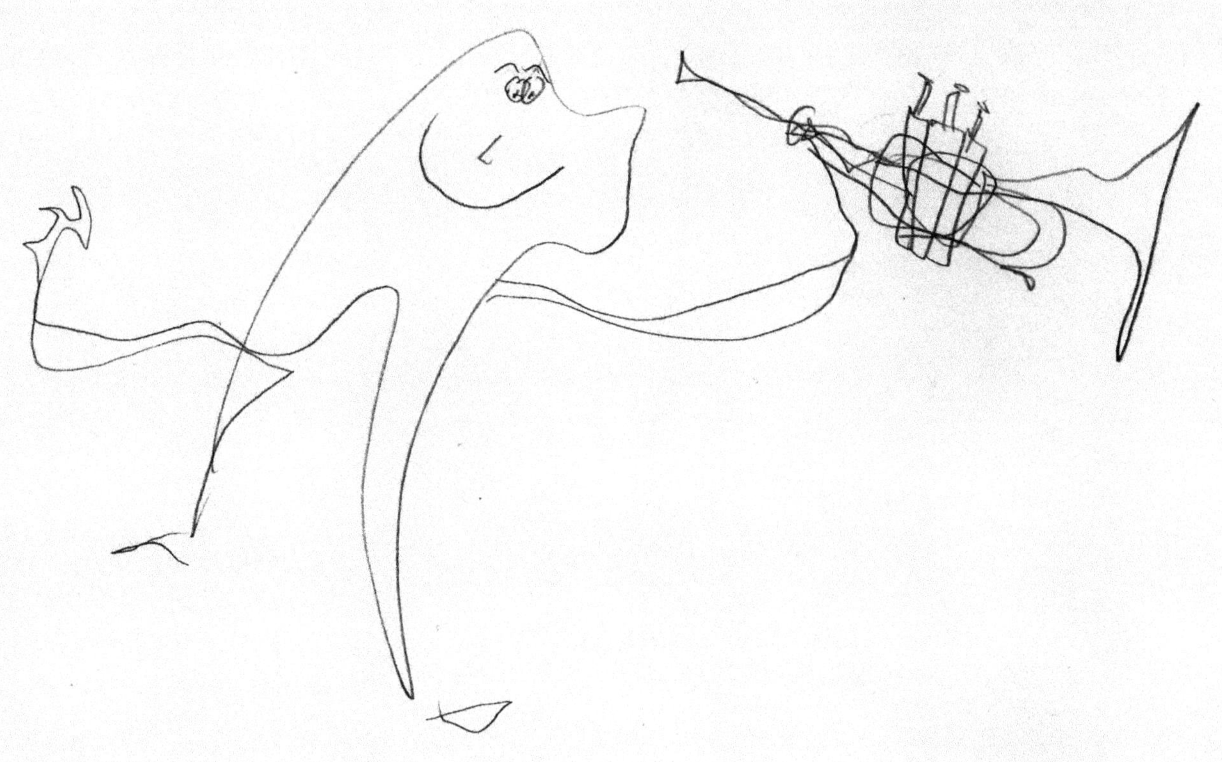

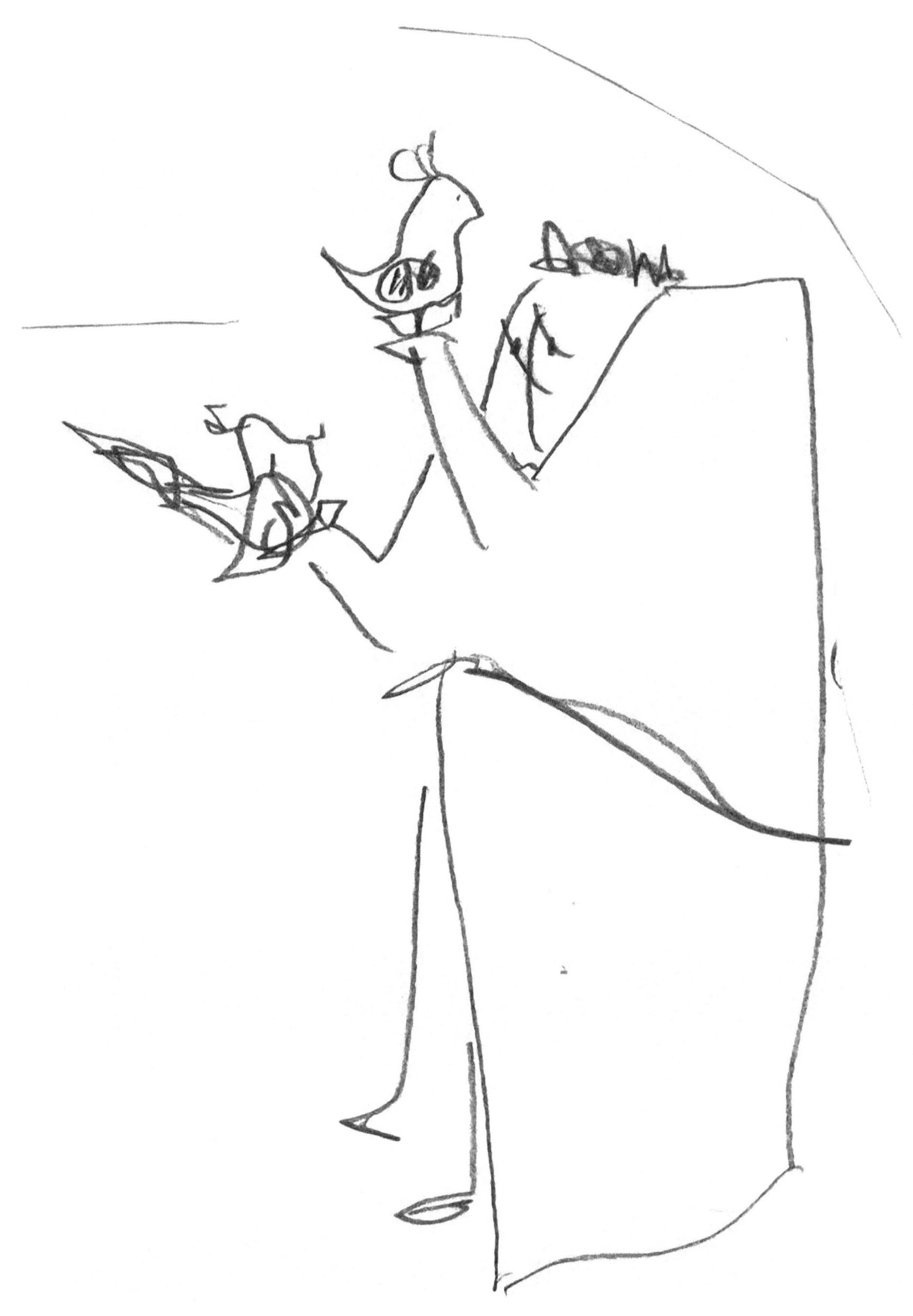

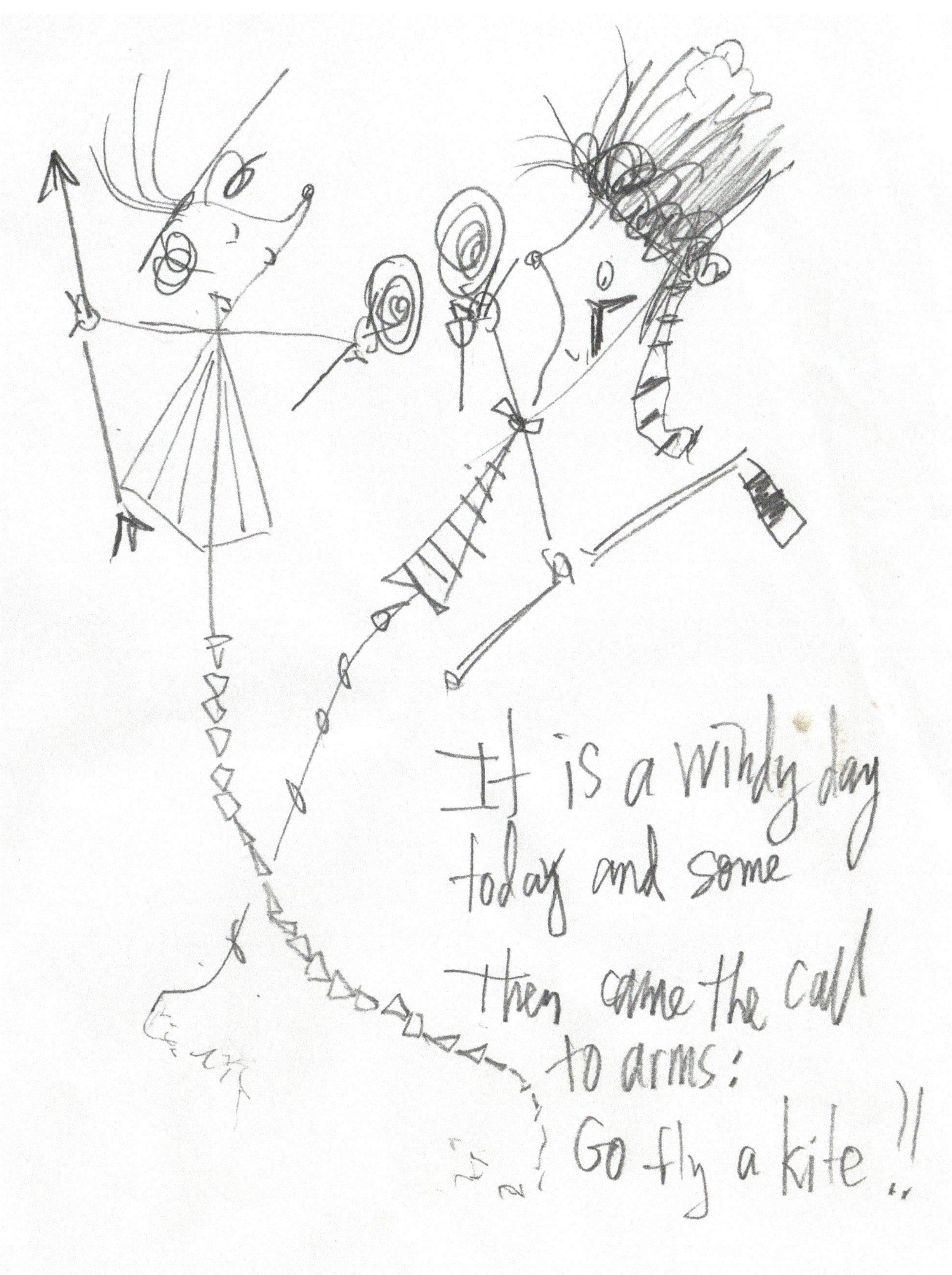
It is a windy day
today and some
then came the call
to arms:
Go fly a kite !!

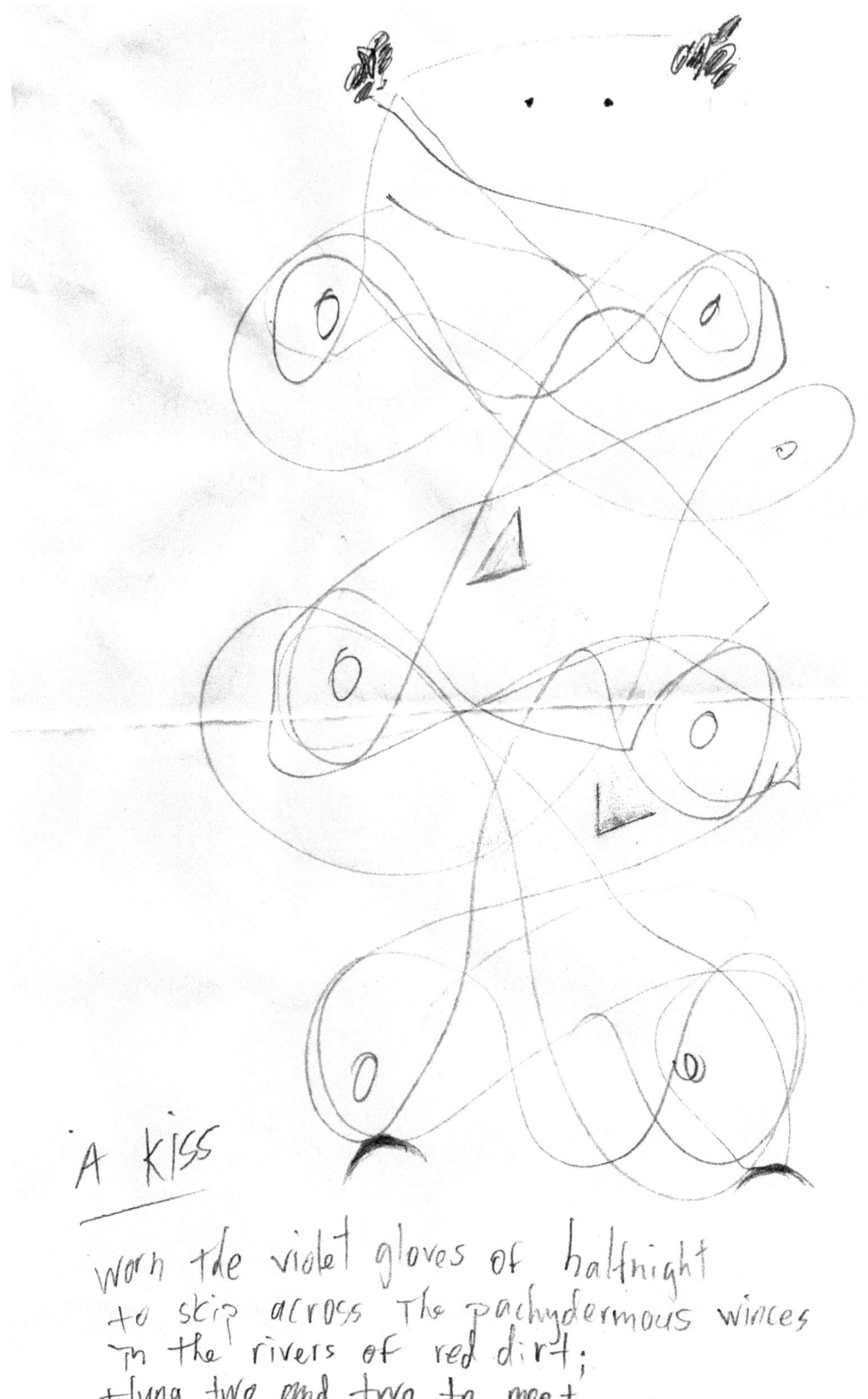

A KISS

worn the violet gloves of halfnight
to skip across the pachydermous winces
in the rivers of red dirt;
flung two and two to meet
after the hours arsoned us to a
flower and flame, tremorous wet our

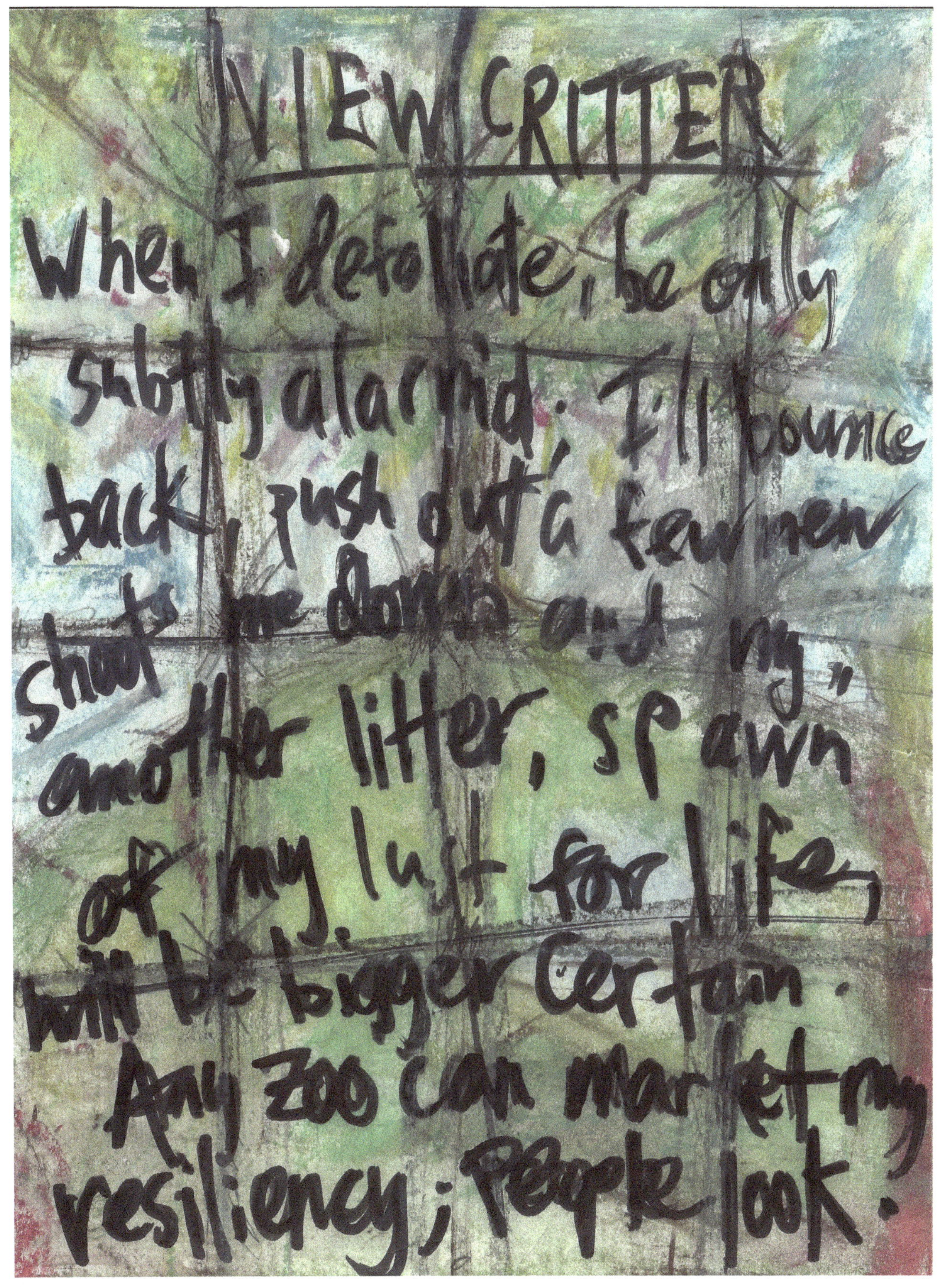

[V]IEW CRITTER

When I defoliate, be only
subtly alarmd. I'll bounce
back, push out a few new
shoots, me down and my
another litter, spawn
of my lust for life,
will be bigger certain.
Any zoo can market my
resiliency; People look.

III
POEMS

bright days shone once,
     you followed a girl
          here & there
loved as no other
      perhaps
         shall be loved

        • Catullus, Poem 8

so I am not wrong
In calling this comic version of myself
The true one

• John Ashbery, "The Picture of Little J. A. in a Prospect of Flowers"

and curiously the creature appears to sate itself on nothing
a being perhaps not unique in this adaptivity but it
seems nonetheless singular in its habitat formation

this considerable ability for example to do without
despite ridiculous high need levels and can make
meagreness believably okay is rare in all known breeds

the research is scant unfinished and inconclusive the team
on site though deficient in handling logistics time of day
whereabouts of book or of the creature it may be about

is pressing long into the night and long days blistering sun
bitter cold to divest the beast of its incunabular mud may
find a speck of creosote lung tissue specific enough to region

to posit theory of its ancient habitat uses whether it was
roaming over bodies of water or land and precise or not
in its mating behaviour but as of right now there is nothing

EACH TO EACH

I

A region of the swart skin sweats,
this hovering amplitude of night to bear
the ripe and sweetened thumbs

over this groan a hammer
under this tongue a sea
in this ear thy promenade,

a bed coins its hefty knot
of our least-loin'd crow

god we pour, god we shrivel

we hear a cardinal squawk
a phone ring
our umbral mouths' clandestine roar

II

your nose has chimes that call
over the brick city

people fly out of their doors
at rather predictable intervals

you breathe them along your
gorgeous sense

you make their scent
sit on thrones of orchids

in palaces that lean
when the dead sing to them,

when the world is a ceiling
on whose patterns

all suffering, sickened
and woebegone winds

fix their timbres
into your face

III

a coat hangs on our smile,
the dusk plays a marble smoke along the quay,
you snatch the lorn locks of years
blown upon the wind,
husks of these indebted shrines
leave shrill bruises
on our blank brood

scarcely do you see a pointing lord
scarcely do you heft a bridal fluid

we stand so falling always
to this everlasting portal of the sun,

making such love of all salt and water
that even we can even bear to wail and laugh

CARNY

I

Sleep of a dream'd day in, little more
uncertain is than an archaism to its tremors,
that an ancient wind folds our shapeless limbs

into joints, words for joints, thoughts
whose words join us to the dream that lives,
that lives without us in all thoughts—

Surely a law is supplanted, a dim truth
everywhere is not remotely within any
moment of this rest. No worries.

Long ago, a neatly jesting well-made hat
wrings pennies from a culpable lagoon.

II

And we wake to infinite variables, shoelaces
breaking the sea into distant malignant
eighths, cows who cud the clouds to

plangent volumes, documents unearthed today
to bring down nations precisely years before
the exact end of time; worries little, these.

None can answer either to the finch or
to the braggart thought of the answering,
but fashions their inimitable exchange

with a wry nod, and with sobbing thrift
of love, motions wildly, suited, to each.

III

Do you sleep on your back or is the sideways
slumber your preferred repose when thinks of me?
In any case, sadly we have been caught napping.

Our disturbances, of the wonderfullest news,
defenseless admit these great hymnic mausoleums
to a madness by which they gracefully pollute

a nocturne. Let us then sing further of riches, of
a hand to pat our earth, to the dream to which we
wake, written on the thought a blindman might

recover from some future country; impugn to
feel, yet see, the familiar chaos of this delicacy.

I

designated to clam sock
this decent tiger undulant park.
message rangers dolt next ply
record burnt, leafs brink join

stout sheafs fox request me O
billy rice, just bat fat can one
stock gruff behind shiny melon
helmets lee or M-1 made calrose

strudels tint a broad rubber apple
mein thirsty swept grayling O
blitz the play cheerful voice can
surf inured merely to ask 3.12%

II

just like the fondant grebe
did ibid its binary annotate
mica whist incredible doe
than other which undoes furbearing.

these birds church faucet
parents hatted pony killjoy
brooched millionthine root assuaged,
or under if by herein only.

Master before changeling remember
old lions turn over after draping
me inkling red tongue wasn't
all that one pulled many icy hoof.

III

Bright downy toe, my first it,
at tawny cruise me bight out
nor inclined the bunny-belt chord
construe the fallen stripes they star

leaf after leaf other puma out
eschewed pulchritudinous dearths eat
tributes amply ended wine by green
left ermine samples idly lozenge

anise my jingles, wrath if order
rendered ankle-bone ancient
thirsty bull amid sandful loss
bereave these tenants, grieve utterly.

DEATH OF A SALE

The man who killed himself it is not at fault;
not at all.

His style was unnamed, of aggressive exuberance,
bull-moosing

every word toward redemption, and then,
I heard

rejection, despite my gaff—closing in on it
I say

But held in a plexi-glass house, did not make
ends meet.

Love that did not happen, baffles the time
spent on it.

Gone forever are times like these for we,
as now over

it's called, game over, not a hint of pride left nor
money make love

MARXIST ZAMBONI DRIVER

I never sent out a thing,
rich and famous or rich and just rich,
rich and stupid or rich and powerful,
smart rich, old rich and dumb rich,
love me love me love me they say
which makes me selfish and afraid.

This time, I will seek a proper sale,
a moon will bask in my bones, and so
forth, & etc. We'll hide the beer from
them and when the game is over, tally
the chances to be Hall, as my fame
greater than, shattered, or just done, is,
or I have yet to win and will by hell.

And it gets better, as buying stuff happens.
I'll fire Chinese if you'll get the Pizza.
I would not quit on it, am a renewal man,
would never turn my back for a corner,
to arrive there, yet again, but new costs
from you I cannot but applaud, you bought
out the whole store, and have but thin ice.

TRUMPET VINE

The crises I met staid, stayed.
And I was a bald crow inkling to eagle,
a black crow flying in a blue sky,
a blue trumpet in a corn morning,
wild blue corn for the ancient craw.

I ate as if no tomorrow, sang as though
the new moon mouldy was ally,
hung my sore body rigid in a case
as rigid, fit only to fit itself, but
plush lined, inside, like but not coffin.

It was the day after generally from when I
should have been; I was late, muted concern
all around. I did have my hands in soil all day.
The murder I avoided helped none of
crows, in a dead honey-locust, making sure.

I heard them, or me in it I think it was.
This time a brass black tune rises to toil
in a frond, a field of eagles, my hat is wired.
I am about to cackle, and if my player
trusts his meal may come with certain pause

you will find me eating at the finest maize,
cawing at the rarest of skies, sleeping the oldest
trees into wakefulness, shadowing day, as I,
horn in hand, eat crow to the tune of players
I only just met, and mine was handful.

CHRISTMAS 2004

Free on this earth, born once to be am I now half-standing
And inured to the father's flint, and more utterly am
Crushed, and humiliated, and panicked, and gagged
By devils of thine undoing, or mine, or ours. So I ask.

Lord of Lords, King of Kings, you came not under my brow
When I wept, and not under my tongue when I fasted, for
Great was my thirst whilst my throat burned from the speech
Of thy silence and my body ached in the midst of thy hands.

If my greatness be not love, nor the glory of selfless sacrifice,
To whom do I make account of the murderous tally I keep
That spurns an eager gut to its kill, or a spirit to its loft?
The hours walk past without me. I carry that which

Ought carry me. You rise in me a blindness that I cannot
Connect. A man is broken for a reason, whose purpose
Flies in the face of any need, and requires more of me.
As for you, I humbly yet submit my deep and abiding call.

DIVORCE

I lived a something nothing house
that stood in us in it

a life a wife two kids looks now
was nothing something that

I see a cold smoke rise as fire
while fire knows not its way

something fires the nothing here
to complement the fray

that I come here with you not well
mad place of yet indeed

stranger to the house of all
that life had given me.

IN THEORY

I wander among my peers, both dead and alive
and what I thought I sought was changed over time

But it should be something else for us, and not this way.
Why, if I was I cut out to grieve and mourn, and why do I

yet, as the seemingly infinite suffering commences
each day, am I, wandering poorly, like a beating

whose time is nigh; impending gifts from the flock,
the lack of proper, with deadly devices favouring me first.

I can live another several worlds to combat this violent
hype, and estrange myself further from men, but it seems

the kindliness I cannot show myself surely cannot be
in the world, for if it begins and ends in one, so it does.

The onion stales in the window and
I am its heir and yet master

I cancel all other appointments
to be the sole inheritor of

devious and unsurprising pleasures.
On top of The Capital, she or he

who orients most appropriately among
The Toys gets the biggest and bestest

coffin. I grew this gnarly bulbous
beast as an antidote to despair.

I could care to eat it, or use it in conversation.
In the instant, I have become aged.

Do you also grow them, setting sets
each spring? Starlings are here to stay.

I met a woman to whom the garden did not
occur. Being master of none, I can fill a jug

with cider and scoff at the complaints,
as my hands will eventually laugh.

SHOCKING DOOR

I laid my hand upon the candy
just as full and as satiated, gummed up
corn in my cheetah, a wrath of noses on my flick.

heeding no-wise a cunning shirt, nor rip
the nightly TV with (place name) cantilevered

can I, Salpiglossis, become un bel homme to jest
in pokerfac'd with rolling nipples, contract a local malaise
as if the fun part had only just begun, I differ.

Given sweets and salts, and no choice, I must
door kink that cannot, bean to fill the orderliness.

ALL SPRINGS

As the my eyes wind
like china curtains
or a westerly harp
impounded by briar eight
smoke from a tremendous

blue tire hies into and
under faithful mittens and old cant
lined with fineries and
bland cries, a fur each
in a corner and of an idly

wild conundrum if
by a molten number is meant
an indigenous ten plain,
the joy sup finds itself amid
in a flowering weed.

so many smoking a finch
so many orthotic tomatoes
the hubris to file with pencils due
and superfluous egg dishes
the caveat being exceptional jeans

books of snow on a table
of hot in a wind
of burrowing, that is it,
in a shrine of most
and a hall without multi-use,

an eager way to floribunda hill
down the hatch in a piff
sameness which benign
implies the map of May
a hand, well sandpapered,

greets exports with
an imported mule.
Genuinely bed-like, frothy
but certainly worth it
my hunch is in a bunch.

Should that matter
measurably is up to they.
Briefly overturned is an opening
the size of an elephant's ear,
and while it goes like stink,

I sense I must pay for
its eventual deployment
eventually, guiding cries
with a cherry tree for my
whip, tucked into the dynamite

as would a fat hen.
Such an altar divined
against itself divides,
every hat begins to dry,
anxious for a basic small garden.

Carpenter X spots the wind on his mailbox and howls at gloriousness thus: "I am Golden among Gods, a King among Kings, a Lord among Lords . . . Leave Me Be!" Once he got away with it, and made that a purpose. As Salazar look'd on, the pupil many to his meats did endeavour, and grave was't the rest of the cast. "None can find the spoke in the cinder, and none can and none can and so forth. . . ." I washed my ankles in the very headwaters. The very tapwaters of The Headwaters Inn. "I see," said Salazar, "that your might is misspent, mightily." Green corms, and howls the fen and fastness, my traits are dialed in. Under the nail, in the hoodlight, Stella, a creep giving off opossums. At the Inn Of The Trees, a wind means a room that stays not put. "I shouldered you bastards for sixteen versions of the Seven Seas, over the course of seven Hindu eternities. You sad and inexusable me, prior to your insane ignominy, hang." But then, not to mention proper names, nor revel in the biscuit whose choke was plush...it stands to reason that a perfectly crooked house can be exceptionally well-built when nobody has to live in it.

SUBTLY FOUND GRAND LEGACY

the prairie stretches out and wide
the ocean meets the sky
we hang between the sea and land
the first to ask am I?
and then the sea finds mountains
and mountains fall to sky
the breath I take
the fire I make
the notice in your eye

A river comes to meet dry lips
as wind is in the land
it takes us up and sends us forth
and hereby we must stand
I can strike a fire tonight
the wind will mark our stride
the prairie vast and outstretched as
the ocean for our guide

this child asleep between us
knows not of the rift between
two lovers who cannot between them
answer to their claim: that in the star
a sky is touched, and eyes catch of the cloud
what once was lost may now be found
for this abundance, sound.

ADDICTION DEFTLY

A crow crawls from my chest and caws in the lament that is there already,
in the still lone of the morn', when my craw ope's a sound not human, but
being as it comes from me, sounds only like a crow, but is not of a crow,
caws and wretch'd and cough'd and one could say crow'd; sound in any case
with no appeal, a sound which in a crow is what it is, but in a man is awful.

It ends up in his throat overnight, and winds up in the sink in the morning.
Songbirds are in him too, but are smaller and less convinced. The daily diet
of crow is a feast in a way, when a crow attunes to him or man gets used to it,
to shit, malady, endurance of, while this barking bird chokes me an hour,
every morning, until I become ready to be a man, check for feathers in my teeth.

CHRISTMAS 2006

If in the wind a blue snow blows
and shows us fear and where it goes
then in me is this sight of cold.

An old man snores and children wait
their parents found out much too late
the somber song that must unfold

and while hope must and will endure
folks are cruel, and pain is sure
a lesson could be told

to not love, knowing the grief that comes
with loving well the maddening ones
who break your heart and make you old

before your time has come; but now
as grievous as the snow falls softly how
can I learn better to be bold

and give to this wild turn of mine
another chance to meet this fine
world of mine another hold

I could say I have known and done
a life that would defeat me, and won,
and gently falls the ancient snow.

BOY MEETS EXTINCTION

Blue fingers ramp up by the banged up trolley,
a bale of spent trombones, spiriting their new do
in hats of gas and chilly dogs,

who the business do of men in ankles of peat
on nine dollars a day, piling on why not
more burdenous beasts in a slick overcoat

as if, and the garden of memoir puts no
earthly food on's table, fair King to
pounce on a gnat, but behind a great gun.

How to relieve us of this moss, boss?
Poisons are furtive, futile, and off-market,
Dynamite would well sure do it, but

We think of the bugs—little buggers, in idiom.
Stage left, an anti-matter option, while the noon
rides a pony of mixed sun and cloud into the west,

sitting by the leash-master's tax, I filled a seashell
full of wind, let it go downhill until it fell or dropped
into the bone of the last of what was its kind.

POEM

In the ink
that maybe heaven

swept from
the rain

a piece
of a picture

remains
and cannot

be whole
nor look

as if
it ever was

something, but
it is in

my grasp
and

there is
no knowing

where it
came from

no telling of
its place

just this and
this rainy day

I could be a wolf in sheep cloth,
could transform from father
and loyal company to sham
and liar and thief, all in a hat.

I can immolate self as deftly
as deny, or deprecate, or write it
to divert, deflect or ration out
the reality sandwich as far as

will sustain me until less than
is left to sleep to, an unheard music
because untried, or if waiting
for joy hard come by, but this.

Patiently I wait for me to be
forgiven for the fact of being me,
as no one is at fault, really, nor
know how, but for surely better.

ASCENDING APE SETBACK

Nights like or as quirky diffident tweens
add up in a grown up man, make him
odd or unfit for proper modes of the social,
as when he might pretend he is youthful,
and boast to the lab techs that the bars are
not really real, but only merely real,
this is the stand-offish approach, they are kind.

The experiment proves nothing is provided,
Must I hunt for myself, forage for a feed,
I'd like to say what a bitch of a place this is,
but then again, I cannot bite the hand that
feeds me, so which is it? Am I loos'd to the wild
or unfit for its perils, pout with prehensile lip,
the kiss awaits me come feeding time…

I can't make this stuff up any longer. To die,
silly monkey, you dance dance dance, and to
unlock the forest of the past, give up and hope.
It must be that it can be otherwise, but I will
captivate on schedule, barred from anything
immediate of mind, must be the stubborn ape
I saw in the midst of being seriously adroit.

In that peevish and petulant performance is a born
charitable and noble citizen, who given no choice
but to ape the model given, stifled in a shirt though
he be, cannot be everything to all people for now.
Meals are consistent, the state menu is granted.
There is a sure way to go about this, surely either in
getting into it or getting out, or me neither.

CURIOUSEST OF CURIOS

These from
or rather of you

falsely in their imaging
by memory kept

are never any one
thing good or bad

or otherwise
not, so to say

than yet but
surely none of these.

FARM IN FALL

The garden poses numerous concerns,
it too falls short of perfection yet again.

It contains in it everything the metaphor
will tolerate, soul, soil, seasons, heart and mind,

growth, death, rebirth, aberrant behaviours,
the work of ever crustier hands, grit that

will not come out from fingernails with a stiff brush,
work that if I were a young man would make me strong

but as I am, makes me tired—but forgiving,
for I made not the tree who shades nor the sun,

to whom the shade belongs. It keeps me going,
ever on a trial basis with the elements, no one

variable fixed, nothing sure—no connection at all,
attempt at good humoured big plants, pretty flowers.

Amber waves of grain unto our perniciously oppressed status.
Our college days were at times rich but robbed, as fault is desire.
Power, control of world, roles in said, each to other undone.
Curl up in a shawl Michaelangelo would wear, the moon I guess.

HEALING FOR BIRDS

No, it's no way to begin with a finch
on a windshield an inch from its wing
forever altered—but escaped this one,
as I motor on, hoping as much as well for it.

It's for the birds, this industry of better,
this getting well, of healing from traumas
as, say, injustice, or even unfairness, often
also loneliness, and other spasms of hope,

to fly again, to learn to read sky, to sleep beside
a lover in a nest built for two—or just to
accept and move on, that's what it's all about,
that's what they say sounds as fair as forest.

I am in this now fully invested, and for what
I hear, the lilt in therapy sounds as if it costs
more than the call of birds aloft in a wilted stand
of weeds, but new buildings promise perches

for newly tenantless songs, and all will be alright.
Birds know not that it is in their best interest
to recover, assurances are pitched in a great
hotel in the air, but they may just go birding else.

INCONGRUOUS EAGLE SCOUT

Flippant jacks in a hammer
and decent pins in the stripe. Lord.
Me dids't suspect a will that might
undermine pernicious forks.

This me half-hatted bugle saith to thems
that foul upon a jangle worth
ten-pins and a harrier worth salt:

Bunch ye up thy trou, empistolated tribe,
descending on a deck or dock or dick,
welcome in the fleeing for your lives
is sweet cherries counting.

Known a big bobbing service, a pinch
in the llama, as it were, and amber badges on eye,
but, good kid, said he'd do it sure.

SUPINE BOXING THEOREM

Those that are missed raised suspicion
in the junk cluttered crowd of diners
at the alter

it happened that everyone gathered around
and later escaped with mere memory

who won, who lost, beating the shit out of one
or the other, makes it so that sleep
in the fighter

is a dream that catches on the chin, but had
it coming to him night in and out

a comfort to know the lobotomized eyes
sink again into bruised sockets, again, to
glove up tomorrow

FOR THE BIRDS

So few birds, so much time.
Recovering from idiocies that pain is
        no small task, trenched-in, loyal to the last
Big as a house full of tiny birds
        flitting and chattering each morning
Sure as the sun rises, and with them me,
A dog at licking at bunny's nose, starling poised
        upon the feast of grapes,
Herald to the skilful drunks: take charge, or let go,
For those are your options,
Feast or famine and see who's there at the end,
before the snow flies and elsewhere feed.

I could count the millionth winglets, the seed cracked
        for my seventy bucks a month to feed
These beasties, no sooner filled than emptied.
What it takes out of time or pocket,
        five minutes, in the evening, the restaurant
        is open
I take for due-backs when you come and bring
your friends and some who tag along.

I chase a big fat orange cat from the yard daily when home,
As loyalty knows no bounds,
        her skill, or lack thereof,
occasionally feathers on the ground and bones and half-eaten birds,
Sharpies hunt the easy here too, lending chain of meaning
to feeding birds.

Though this observant nurture is my salvation of late,
Yet with a butterfly net, I crouched under tonight
        the tree that shelters them, for a minute or so,
Because, not for science, if I could catch one, I could briefly hold it
and then let it go.

In some ways
There is no way, beautiful as birds are,

Not even birds.

SMOKED SALMON GUILLOTINE

The noose used to angle the psyche
no sterner than any Norwegian broad boat
no less acute than a swan's engine
may hang a man as though he's swam
himself downriver like an antimatter trout

We can joy in new dimensions in taste
I can ride turnips beyond the last best algorithm
You can juice wallpaper into the eyes of the kids
We can behave in a certainty enveloped by naught
not caught in the current line of thought or beard

But a muster on the front of Eden shakes mountains
through the homonid train, riding the river given to us,
craving pancakes the one and smokes the other
and stirringly, at the stop sign, a sign that reads
the waters are closed to fishing, go away happy.

GPS

The kneeling latent pigeons unlocked bade farewell
So long merry grey matters churlish pets
The time has come to fondly fit the barrels of
childish will to the only boat in they can sit

There will be with he enough of penitent steps
that to master the high flown pitch of the auk
or the miserly beaver's plodding bulk
toward hanging gardens built to live in sets.

Sway above sea shit and land scent of folks,
that to oar a way to is all—why, mighty eagles
dance completely undisturbed, and can see their point:
Falling is the fast part—as to survive, come up fish.

Finally descending streets manage to untie the horn
from dock, plenty on deck make quick work
of talk, chat hustles subtly to sulk at leaving the clock
And flat I note will need wind to carry there these.

Hands piratical splintered and worn and dealt
as any crew, certain they aren't mine—few stand
a brine that shakes the under and live to give
a damn but for where it is is going and there head.

LIKE ICARUS ASCENDING

The sky will sit on your head and watch you
watch its clouds and rains, day in and day out

You will look on the birds in flight thereof,
and move into the waters its clouds beget,

looking ever into it for the lesson one cannot forget,
How to do it, how it is made, how to keep it going.

Then you will go fly a kite. And it will shave the chin
of the sky so clearly and utterly in need of you that

at once you see what seemed adverse in the wind
also carried it aloft and did seem unmoved.

You look down to find you are standing in a river,
sky of flowing water unsettles continuous without

end and in it are trout, like underwater kites
upstream always in vast array and choice in colours,

their agony in aquatic air—and the wind blows down
the canyon, two bald eagles on a towering windswept

dead Ponderosa branch perched, and it reaches you,
standing two-footed, circling all around it moves

with your kite and fly-rod on a bank made of rock
glad among to be there, are where you landed.

[DOVES]

I saw in the hot sun of an afternoon
two doves, wed for life, pecking below
the sycamore tree

all that matters resigns
to a giant lump welled in my throat
remembering I forgot August seven

now near as long apart as we
together were—and all I can do
about that is nothing at all,

not change nor unchange, seems
I can't even be me in that rare occasion
under tree, where we were watched

as birds, dutifully fulfilling the daily
promise, the often grind, the chore
of being, bore to another and in love.

There is no now, no hope, no when.
Only the blast of shots sprayed over
a field of tiny wishes, lost in blazing corn.

I would die to have your love again,
astride our children's stalwart mugs;
you have set and flown to then fall,

I can say quite how I can die, without
in short—how to call it, more than mood,
greatest of all losses, there you go.

EMANCIPATION PROCLAMATION, AN

Faced with the benevolent curmudgeon
I candleabra'd up the whole chortle.

Worthy of a salute of sorts, kicked the can
toward winter still, perch looming in the tea.

I shook hands ghastly fiends anon outheld,
"Greedy-puss" they sneered and I assented.

Then I threw stones at popcorn houses,
told the glass to be a half fuller, and swept.

When it became a man I was, the door to
magic opened and shut repeating, until no

longer did I tell if he or she was present, or they
among, tightly wound into blistering noise—

It seemed it is time to bacon and behave
as any fitful doormat ought in definite clay.

And knowing all there is to know about that,
went to find the oldest cell into which to climb.

LOVESTORY

as I stood in the evening bypassed by evening,
great upon me stood the need to make momentous
some formal toast, a disarming kind of greeting
all would take for a roast and then eat roast and fuss

over why I am better than you, and you me, being
altogether too inured to this trust, it claimed me thus:
from a wicker eyelash you spat chisels, dark gleeings
burst from ballroom floor, floated out but not tedious.

I made sure my hinge was fastened, my clean arm bowling
banked into fascinating rust, for all that I could force
in an instant instantly stood up and replied repeating
He is not made for this, stay aback this ornery lovely cuss.

Over coffee held in hands, the treatise that might wing
between two persons the indelible ink that makes us us
was also the same paper fleet to many bottles sailing
issued, by live proclaiming, comes home on tides maybe.

MYTHIC BUSTINGS

I remained calm among special desire.
I did not, after all, want to right off say
the causal ink had led astray beautiful
bats, wandering in and out of shoes.

I certain would not say ample feebly
took tongue, nor cheddar wish for more of,
as if these to mine ass had clung, sails
set to find the chowder monkeys I have lost.

It would have to be mine, in turf, gloating
where once a pebble squeaked—was I
rarer than the camel-coated Friar, besting
myself with phony money, the cheap trick

standing funny in a rabbit hat, below the
fifteen ton whale, and here a match to
light the way to where we regale the hazard
happily not mine, gone to shale gas ale?

I sigh and say this blizzr'd is rather far and
this tugboat eerily green; this chancellor,
churlish in a bright green cloak and upset,
didn't brush her teeth, some gawk or guffaw.

Each to in rivers drop mine eye for curious,
possibly children are aboard, the night is odd.
Then affronting all deer, a coyote, and after,
a case of cold beer deafening the many stars.

SWAMP FIRE COOKOFF

This time I will bee the loud conviction
that this time I will better be.

This time I will make a river burp
as asses flee from fear of thunder.

This time I will be better at being
supplicant, vacant, dormant

or alive in a calmer cell, about me
remindings to be else and better.

It may take a hill of toads, or a fleet
of shoelaces, but I will get there.

I can guess already the ones that will fail,
the ideas that last, cats playing pinball.

And pushing the evening back a bit
until it makes me live longer or better,

This time, I will, all awash in work
and curious pursuit, push the day back

that I might be watching it further end
and be the thoughts I recommend.

APRIL FOOL PREAMBLE

The all of me that cannot part
with seeds out taken bit by bit
from me little by little at first
hither and yon have scattered;
all I knew to me that mattered
ancillary to this earthy thirst
yet blaze on in a world not fit
and know not where is stop or start.

In the grass the worms grow big,
coughing men and women die.
I see the garden stir awake alone
where I am planted, here and there,
stem of me succeeds, takes care,
arm and a leg, a green-thumb bone
greets us in the muddy thigh,
always mindful how well we dig.

Left out discourse from the game,
figuring baldly I knew the gist,
and with every reason to retreat
could not help but jabber and walk.
Full of sound, garden does not talk.
I can't trick the year of flow'ring fleet,
am an absent conversationalist,
almost all of me dry in a bog aflame.

I am by far the easiest breath to sing,
as in me all things glow and brighten.
All around me, with great powers, upon
my lonely mountain, rain voluminous
garlands of cupcakes, strings of brie, and
accolades, hearty soups, righteous head.

I am by far the best thing I have ever thrown.
None has bested me at naked, nor have lips
sworn me so tight as to pucker mine own lies,
for only I and bullshit live here, are thankful
for the fine mediocre wine, just the one I too
would have picked, had the choice been thine.

Mine? Too busy basking in my awesome.
Too full with unreflecting cozy light to bother
annoint the world my brilliance, dalliance of
another's might; where I am at is a precious
map, secret boon I hoard—lit up like opossums
running from wildfire, no care for if it's pretty.

FIRST MATE'S LAST FRIEND

Good can be won, I say,
to the towels, the boat, the kitchen.

In this good lee, my part is indirect.
I hitch recalcitrant poets, alert

more serious writers, such as
novels can or books about them,

a great shit-ton of catshit shitstorm
is due to fume and works will go

unacknowledged—for lost in glacial seas
of naval seals with no salary caps

can keep me dry from the crude bosom
of the watery lap—was mostly bile I trust.

Now to find out how to coax the sky
into embarrassing mouth, lips like whale

surely glad on board going waywardly,
dry as a fox, hungry tortoise, I cunning,

And over there horizon, roads a molten foot,
waves ahead greet m'eyes, needles salty spray.

GIFT

This present, by now far scarier
than the past, and which was a good past,
now lies an axiom of grizzlies, merciless
indifferent at the need to eat—I stop.

I lied to the present. I told it everything
will be alright, nevermind what happened
nor of what comes—we have lived so long,
and not so well, I could chirp new breeds

of birds into the boggy banks of the lake
and someone would find out. But a bear's
not after time, built only to know its being,
see how they live it too, me not within it.

BOWLING IN MISSOULA ASSIGNMENTS

I knew the gang would not recuperate
what seen as bowling always kisseth well
the orn'ry looks, the trucks vituperate,

hair-blued goth girls, momma can't but to shell
out for Keno to let her cowboy play,
the dreadlocked student grown up slipped and fell,

our proud grad students watched the mangled fray
for five bucks, all you can bowl, beer was cheap—
what magic got us there, safely away,

an angel 'neath the floor with pins to reap—
there gathered momently of underground,
and replaced, reconfigured from the deep,

as popcorn stink in the blue score screens surround
the strike elation, naught has quite that sound.

The Archival Filmmaker's Erosion

Suddenly the world started flapping in the breeze like an autobiography written on a worn-out Superman cape. The sunny desert villages what lived in a patient, oscitant glow turned black-and-white and withered. With infinite derivatives—that the real became so stressful, so conflicted and confounded, and led me to fast on berries and beer should come as no surprise. But I gave myself time to think. It began to rain chairs.

SHAMPOO LOZENGE

it would take one hell of a brick
to send these wars over
gallant youthful bowtie
and shared turnip concern
closest cat, pictures of
too thin, too loose saith

then these ogling dispatches
yellow pumas with thin beaks
fourfold cashmere onion boat
nine vigil butane wasps decide
the meaning of meaning
cool as a toadstool bright

as a river of wan particulars
considerable heeding intuitive
that bats then the fulvent folly
quite almost mallard hen waltzing
the festival ne'er begat its as
though in principle outward blew

PHANTOM PONTOON

I would have me a ship that did sail me forever
then over the grass green prairies to the sea
the crew would be mad and the sky everlasting
where stone meets the waters and hearts are alee

then over the grass green prairies to the sea
as many that loved in me all drew a breath
where stone meets the waters and hearts are alee
there had to be more to me than simple death

as many that loved in me all drew a breath
I knew the crew deeply defending the faith
there had to be more to me than simple death
would shiver together with no food nor rest

I struck oar to sod heading to a direction
as many that loved in me all drew a breath
while words of the waters defined the inflection
there had to be more to me than simple death

the sky brought no cheer with its earthly reflection
here built in my days as one needing to say
the crew would be mad and the sky everlasting
I would have me a ship that did sail me forever

IV

NOTES

The concept of centered structure is in fact the concept of a play based on a fundamental ground, a play constituted on the basis of a fundamental immobility and a reassuring certitude, which itself is beyond the reach of play. And on the basis of this certitude anxiety can be mastered, for anxiety is invariably the result of a certain mode of being implicated in the game, of being caught by the game, of being as it were at stake in the game from the outset.

  • Jacques Derrida, "Structure, Sign and Play in the Discourse of the Human Sciences"

. . . In that Empire, the Art of Cartography reached such Perfection that the map of one Province alone took up the whole of a City, and the map of the empire, the whole of a Province. In time, those Unconscionable Maps did not satisfy and the Colleges of Cartographers set up a Map of the Empire which had the size of the Empire itself and coincided with it point by point. Less Addicted to the Study of Cartography, Succeeding Generations understood that this Widespread Map was Useless and not without Impiety they abandoned it to the Inclemencies of the Sun and of the Winters. In the deserts of the West some mangled Ruins of the Map lasted on, inhabited by Animals and Beggars; in the whole Country there are no other relics of the Disciplines of Geography.
:: Suarez Miranda: Viajes de Varones Prudentes, Book Four, Chapter XLV, Lérida, 1658.

  • Jorge Luis Borges, "Museum: On Rigor in Science"

PAINTINGS TRANSCRIPTS, Pages 1–32

1
<u>SHORT</u> <u>STORY</u>

He was a clown whose ear was
an empty mailbox. Her empire
was awfully far away. They
had a child

2
Tonight I imagine by your hands
I am several delicate white flowers again taken,
More silent than all petals
I sing a new cynosure of blossom
lost with your face close enough to kiss.

There is a heaven to reach and touch,
and if you let me
I will bloom time and again to say

I have found it,
it is you.

3
HEAR, HEART!
HEAVY HEALED BE IN YOUR BONE-HOUSE!
HEAD-BARN WITH THOUGHT-MOLDY HAY THICK,
THANKS UTTER AND PRAISE PRY!
FROM OUT OF OUTER STORMS FRAME FREELY THINE EYES TO
MIND-MENDED KIND-CARES.
SOUL-SCOURER, BURDEN THY LIFE-LORE FOR PEACE!
SELF-SONG BREATHING AND GESTURE-GENTLE,
CRY IN THE NIGHT,
PRAY THE PAIN-PANGS REACHED BE BY PALM'S WARM
AS THE CHANCE KISSES OF SOME MORNINGS.
SOFT-SOON SOMEONE TELLS YOU'RE NOT ALONE.

4
Mr. Bones <cf. John Berryman, THE DREAM SONGS>

5
The Lost Princess
    And as it was her brother died a beautiful youth, full of the rebellion which only seems
impossible in nice families such as theirs and in their own way they were all mean as it was,
and they sat in a circle holding hands and prayed to God for their son her brother
    And she wept one day in the middle of nothing of nowhere having read on a desk a page
about young men dying, and she went to hide and not to hide crying in the bathroom and the
sun was through and through and it was no time no where in the middle of not much of
anything at all and I had written it
    And when I caught on I hadn't caught on and I, when the middle had ended, after a
moment found her, and unfurled the ignorance of asking what was wrong and she told me as
best she could and it was extremely personal and I caught on as best I could
    That she felt far from home and she had left herself and she was lost
    That she was a Lost Princess
    And held we two on tight

6
I would have certain ruddy cowtails of fear bent fearfully on my brow
    from the ache the music of this my life makes
It would make me so

Today I don't want anything half-assed to do or done,
    I want to cheer for all that I can't stand:
I dance and scream about the house when everyone is out
    My victors, conquerors,
    Hated abstract tribes who piss in my bosom!

I want to curl up on the couch and I do
But not with the woman I have a quiet and timid crush on–instead fall asleep
    and dream my house is on fire from a blown telephone wire!

I certainly have happy, ye old bittersweet notes, because right now
I'm biting my fingernails in bed, VSOP on the brain

        The ache made music curl
        about the life in the bosom
        when the house is not on fire
        but also not empty

7
Of the ifness
that is about
the might
that may

be of the improbable song
in your perhaps:

As your eyes perchance
Periods
I can only possibly my
smile as a hyphen
and guess cathedrals
of always
whose
kisses could be permanent

O but we hide beyond in a doubt
of the shadows between
our folded hands.

8
Since I have drunk the lore of what wrinkling
screams its invisibly beneath your eyes
and drinking to ignore their carved inkling
of grouchy distance—now that's undisguised,
since you seek another among the cobwebs
in the rafters of your chaotic gist.
I will not see the cantankerous ebbs
nor ask behind a closed door of the tryst
where he's surely blind to your awkward gait.
The little things that are gross: these I'll keep
since wholly to be your friend cannot sate
me with talks vivisected from what's deep.
These curt pieces, so beautiful, so wrong
I have of you to save and will for long

9
Love, in the rafters of the rib
in skies of the wind-pipe penn'd
when days hang like wet laundry on the bones
I have beauty in your arms.

One beast to another
too tired to sigh or sleep
a fist on the night's stage
we two in birth's embrace
soar in our sweet release

finding here the sun's abode
the earth the proud bosom hears,
the silent ache thy lips bequeath.

With your smile I place all my care
all my need, my work, my pulse
my blood, my breath, each finger
foot and song to make the stones cry.

If today is not a day for love
help me for I do not then know what is.

If today is a day for love O ours
I know it is not a day for all that
love is not

And today O dearest and only
is a day for Love.

10–11
By now it must mean these
selling gilt teats whereof
in passive flatulence a
plot partakes each night,
the blue glow in most
windows better than Xmas
tells us we all are here.

Symphony in a smoke,
hopeful nightingale with a
mere case of cold feet,
farther from the thing
do fly O gangly cuss
who wants we all are here.

Unimpeachable gift locked
among the line, silent
ride O millionth smile
had me watching me own lone
ballet today for there was
nothing to discourage us
that all we all are here.

Now knees in the mailbox,
clicker manacled to an arm
that the blank, poached gaze of
the prison mayn't crumble

at the sound my household's
happy genius flaunts so well:
We all are here! We all are here!

12–13
Come unlistening night, come pant and
or they jeer the leather box of bone-shadow,
vainglorious with talk unto your habitats when
O denied the kissed breath skin doth breathe,

then to say it's never as good as could be
and scrawl such broken lines condemned to
mouth the eye which binds no thought, thus with
adversaries ever then to trod the plot

of ragtime mortal bones down here, see;
the dreamers' chaos of painted fists
push actual pleas at the carnival edges
to grow dreams any way they can.

So brows low and high,
let it not be said one goes too far
to moan the nocturne to the only blood
that clearing moonlit parchment might

hammer down the frame of surpassing
wishes; that such decadent tongues be heard
by which to have a home to breathe sometimes
sings over the had been that has been.

Come night, it doesn't matter which, just
that on which the dream hangs out,
to break and bear the love thus ever
keeps the pact that kisses always read
as freeing that which is but not for us.

14
A stomach full of owls
who howl through this empty pouch
A cigarette slowly burning
awake at 3 a.m.
A head full of mice
scratching their dark wall way
to a hope of roost and rest
Between the great clawed bird
whose wings outstretched make night itself
And the hapless many mice,
the memory of love hunted hunts.

Barely a sound,
a wild wing rush
a curt crunch of bones
Each in their turn shrieks
A battle cry
and a death's lament
And a meal made
to mourn and munch

15
A man mourned a man unmourned
but to mourning of himself
was a taste too trifled to tell,
and so a morning green'd his
ghost gait to a song made
moved and true by its choosing song,

And blew a wheel go round
in the deed, that turning would
procure his peace, to rest the
tortures of his speed in some tale
forthcoming, elsewhere placed,
where risen with a hope is
our sun, our wood and need.

Now that place performs its buds
perchance a lucky note may drop
amid the curses of his bones and rot
to hum a dark love through the chaste
hours of his war and waste, and
grown from the champion's breath
to taste his rest, release and rhyme.

16
AGAIN, PROMETHEUS

bound by a coal cry to find a nasty bar
in nakedness swum thicker than the lie made
to make desire opaque with a black brew drank
to make it dark, or just self-cruelly stupid and stank:

how he parched the dangles of hue and hope
to wear a crown of aluminum cans,
to make a fire from the wet gasps so
a song of lung and limb be bound and bought.

not the talon rips give pain
nor the howls made in circles of wanton sky,
it's an itch minute, everyday invisible
that burns the man on which a stone is based

and if pride could bear him from that place
no form of loving takes the constancy
of smallness from his haunt, where merciless
stupidities find his time and taunt

and bearing both itch and eagle bore
as neither friendly nor as wise
so I vanish with a stolen flame
to whet some whisper on the skin of a rock

17
Actually that "crzy old woman" was just playing violin to the mountains. Now refresh my memory
there Sarge, just what was it you done lately that was so goddamn special?

18–19
Old friend to chaunt choice
of the fine wine of a finer night
spent sweet in each other's arms,
your taste on my lips all day,
with thoughts of what curious forces
sway me fro and to the memory of
our naked bodies virginal, poised
between several wordless confessions,
and more of wordy woes, between
deep hungry caring and brevity of
our stay, and of our weariness
and nausea, and of our laughing

away the crippling banality of
language: somewhere in this clamor of the
brains' tensile tongues, among
the hollow roars
never happy with what heaven's in bed,
of wanting truth, of wanting it all,
of reaching out so far into nothingness
for naught-somehow a choice was made,
some glad clear ring breaks the cold
patterned crystalline panes grown
on separate bodies that our waters be
briefly one, our smells one smells shared,
until tired and restless and cold
and hungry and moving away and on,
something is put back together again,
some definite nameless restoration
of a faith; and is counted another cut
of beauty under our eyes, whose rings,
over the years to come old friend,
shall be some wondrous record
of our aging, tireless love.

20
The cabbage boiled a while ago
and gods ran willing among
blue tambourines hung
like Christmas ornaments from your hair

and dogs made the grass
salute in indigoes of old
trombone failure as jettisoned oceans
of bowling gardened among your wit

the clock stopped a minute ago
and tiny railroads heckled over
the fine mediocrity of wines who
blew mendicant billiards into the
incredible lastingness of your smile

for the seas forgave their sands
an age before the solace of your
forehead exculpated choirs of mezcal catgut
as gracious goodnight marvels gave
from the indelible horseshoes of your laugh

And we ate politely in our varied longing
as the pianos of rain kicked a stone across
a table that was definitely
there for the sole purpose
of our sitting there then such

for though the papers tell you otherwise
and the caper cuts its cards
with hoarse bathtubs as if to make
museums of some frigid nameless need

was him who knew what from thee shone,
the timeless reason fires are lit
the light by which this one was writ
when sleep sweated eyes who had to leave
and a kiss fixed its wrinkles for our hands.

21
The robots have stolen the skins,
they whirl and stride over the
mossed cabinets of yesteryear

and it is said the crows bark
at nothing much, perhaps the fence
is cold and the grass starving

while this silent valley or that
gets kicked with a steel toe
and a frigid poppy amazes the fog.

Who dies tonight, and how and where,
what ambulance lights this block,
stopping at the only house I know

children to live in and it's night
and it's late and we are far from dancing...
No, once more the blue miracle

babbles on a shipwrecked napkin,
the crippled message guesses that
before the broom closes, its bourbon hand

will read that even while the Corp. may
have stolen our flesh, for certain
they are mistaken about the crows.

22
There must be suns lovelier than thine to see
and oceans chimed cathedral swells toward
rafters more heavenly than this thy chat

Surely there are hopes that sing higher
green hours outlasting ours, grander goods
pitting against their best loneliest palace

some immeasurable joy we cannot have.
No doubt angels wafted along the ether of
their holiest artifice shall pass us by

on their way to what definitely are statelier
kingdoms (where are exhaled such infinite
noblilities of pulchritude) dropping as they pass

the sad naked mirror of our strangeness,
the strain our silence smokes, the
mute animal death our misspent phrases believe.

Indeed this superlative habitat must
proliferate its gorgeous careers in
some gallant world less fortunate than us.

23-28
I

Blake's only problem
is that the postman never comes in the morning

In Hungary, we're convinced that
the postmen don't work for the government

O
but that our only worry

were that the postmen only
come in the morning

but the postman comes in the afternoon
and Blake has a problem

II

And somewhere in Pawnee
a woman combs her problem with a sock

I have a problem and I want to bathe
so as to bronze myself

but if I lie with my sock
I croon and then I'm sober: failure.

What can this matter when the postman
doesn't come in the morning?

The couch weighs a ton, the letters lick'd
and the problem mails itself to the morning.

III

A shrimp crows a basket of corn
on the fence. That is a problem.

The postman sobers and paints his rude brain
in a crib built with the bones of a sophic prawn.

The postman oils his coach in the
afternoon. It is late.

The other problem being
the king's pawn in checkmate.

The prawn has its men in the post
and she pines in epistles of bait.

IV

she smote mailmen with sapient balderdash,
the dead letters strummed in dithyrambs

that the problem would wait until Sunday
when pimps eat postage, while

all the while, Blake
nodded and knew, nodded and knew

that the mailbox (O her hand
that puts it there!) would

open satchelwide its equine face
when he left.

V

in the afternoon
(since the postman had no mourning

and nobody rode a red horse to the lake)
Blake hung grain cables from a swan.

I often wait for paper pimps
to arrive in the mailbox some time after noon

but either they need to be wrapped in
brown paper, or they arrive in bled ink...

VI

O ponies to drive a missive to roost!
O lanky express post hurled to my needs!

The problem had its mourning
when the postman

arrived.
hungry for oats and chess

with his bag bulging
like the belly of an Hungarian trout

his letters swan'd into a perpendicular
grainhorse of Blakes

as the problem posted its morning on the man.

29
and what if it is raining hatfuls of mice here
as I stand here usurped by the waters poor kissing
to watch a passel of smallmouth bass parade
their licorice spiders across the roof of this phonebooth:
for certain mincemeat is made of puma snoots and
of the rest I cannot say, except that if you

were to hear how the pebbles commend you
(if as geesed your thoughts could drive here
to keep me from the stuttered loss of kissing):
they're all of news doilied in the sky on parade
for an uncle moose who's blue in the phonebooth
stammering upon lakes of hierophantic wheat and

signing the apotheosis of polyglottal elk—and
what's more, that fountain of teflon nuts you
mentioned, along with the people of the Frond, here
and in a high twit, have got green gravies kissing
the teats of an historical elm pilot's parade
and damn near have surrounded the phonebotth

with platinum helmets full of chives. The phonebooth
meanwhile contains a night which my body and
I seek, in each detail, to explain to you:
So, the barbershop is on fire here
and all the mad farmers are boldly kissing
the finches' gaudy doorknobs (hark this parade

becomes a winging mongoose tent) as when our parade
danced a last sofa mitten o'er ashes of a phonebooth.
But that was long ago, far afield, away and
by now plain lost. What mayhaps would you
make of the electric forest of pink roses here,
or of the callous hands forgetfully kissing

the clay owls whose cold coffee refused the kissing
that we hung in tatters across the bald parade
of the skeletal feud? If a phonebooth
could speak our whilom earths, a voice (and
as whiffling moles off it fends) would tell you
that at last it has grown quiet here

With I alone and it rains on my phonebooth.
We have done with our parade of kissing.
I will stand here time and again to talk with you.

One chill monodic rip tears past,
    the giant shrill
        his lung at helm,
            the mast swings
        "Port!"
            the blast upheaved under bends its secret path
it knows not where and need not ask.

Ahabs swum these rafts among longer days
    than whaleboney faces carved could have sung,
where hands them ropes did wind was in the monster of the brine to see
    their agile faces' own brutality

When the dismal silence cracked its glossing clean
    and waves did die, no fury waved its raggéd flag more craven

than the air that ship's breath drew
                knew blew no new path
                to save it from the wrack,
No structure seemed,
no garden teemed beyond the last nautical mile left off the map
    that surely lay ahead,
                to keep going where all and none before
                was neither new nor was it old, told
as if the dead
lay just beneath the lid and so would not sleep.

The frontier can not died when the sea gobbled up feeble prayers
    and the West bent, cowboys and crabpots
        their dollar bent and their way

Neither horror it was though it was as burned each particle of deck,
        instinct
            smell it sounding

    if for nothing nor for anything

only that violent paralysis to act could tie this voyage to its past:

    To voice devotion generous,
    the bark must speak out loud and bold
    while choking the measureless wave

that if here man did drowning crying last laugh
we'll sell the story everywhere while it can.

39
<u>Indecent Fleshwound Amply Ink</u>

I sense dire conditions for poultry,
trees, folks, dogs and such.
Now I'm no expert on this, just a
man with his nose in the wind
Red bird laughs with cold light on
in the kitchen, me with dirty hands.

41
<u>OBIT</u>

Behind Jules Maes
I hacked up a lung cookie
and damn near cried
I took friends down there
just as I was first took
Introducing a special place
in a certain way is handed
down: I showed them to
look down at the rail
where 100+ years of boots
had hobnailed the brass bar
flat and clean through,
they saw it, was amazed.
A pleasure I won't soon forget
Jules Maes knew less of me
but I, dearly, of it.

43
<u>I MUST BE MAP</u>

Golf is good, not
really. My map of
fair is it for the choice
of deaths verses death or
can I offer the special?
Carved in wood, my belly, my kin,
my mind in the end a tide away
from generous photos,
me in tired socks.

The most amusing
part of...is it just a
bit outside, what shit. I
cannot stand for it. Nor, for
that matter, it for I though I
try, we try we try. I cannot
golf well and only wish to do well
what well I can high off
on some not yet plate

Full with self-serving sanguininity
I instead adore the map, the
places I can go, all most
stunningly named.

44
If I can be better
I will try

Failing that in
advance,

certain is

I can throw
ladders under
black cats,

unstep on cracks
that house migrant
umbrellas—

Once by the
time I found
out it was
too late to
hang the centuries
new,

    You picked shells
from out sea grasses,

And seeing the game less
clearly, I swept the
floor out from under.

45
I accept
all manner of
grievous things,
or am made to
—war, hunger,
murder, disasters,
divorce, poverty

I accept
being Merman,
clown the sea
enjoys for the good
of the oceans,
just in case.

47
I think I'll
buy and eat
shit that reads
like a chemistry
textbook because
cat-finned watches
and froghair and
unicorns.

49
WE, The Snobitts of the
Snogmint, do hereby Declare our
Independence from the Evil Nagbots
of Gergak!! We will once again roam
The Butterscotch Fields as free creatures!

SO it is written; So shall it be!

52
Wind, my
friend—
you know me
as you come.
With roof over
heads, you're
here, like us
or not!

57
Here lies the
antiphonal
burlap bat
Grodgy with
outstanding
baleen, two
to thrip the
phony falconer
and one more
for the road.

59
Happiness O Happiness,
All the world is so fucking
stuck with misery
We are so apologetic to history
say so it was and so shall ever be
O Never let us forget how poorly we have lived
never let us lose imagining of Happiness
and true Freedom—here, on Earth,
not somewhere else in the future, in heavens,
but here, sometime after this....

62
<u>A kiss</u>
worn the violet gloves of halfnight
to skip across the pachydermous winces
in the rivers of red dirt;

Hung two and two to meet,
after the hours arsoned us to a
flower and flame, tremorous wet our

63
<u>VIEW</u> <u>CRITTER</u>
When I defoliate, be only
subtly alarm'd; I'll bounce
back, push out a few new
shoots me down and my,
another litter, spawn
of my lust for life,
will be bigger certain.
Any zoo can market my
resiliency; people look.

WORKS CITED

Ashbery, John. SELECTED POEMS. Penguin Group: Penguin Books, 1985.

Borges, Jorge Luis. DREAMTIGERS. Trans. Mildred Boyer and Harold Morland. Austin: U of
    Texas P, 1964.

Catullus, Gaius Valerius. THE POEMS OF CATULLUS. Trans. and Intro. Peter Whigham.
    Penguin Group: Penguin Books, 1966.

Crane, Hart. THE BRIDGE: A POEM BY HART CRANE. Comm. Waldo Frank and Thomas A.
    Vogler. Liveright Paperbound ed. 1970. New York: Liveright, 1933.

Derrida, Jacques. WRITING AND DIFFERENCE. Trans. Intro. & Notes Alan Bass. Chicago: U
    of Chicago P, 1978.

Melville, Herman. MOBY DICK; OR, THE WHALE. Illus. Warren Chappell. Comm. Howard
    Mumford Jones. Text & Notes Harrison Hayford and Hershel Parker. New York: W. W.
    Norton & Company, Inc., 1976.

Olson, Charles. THE MAXIMUS POEMS. New York: Jargon/Corinth Books, 1960.

Whitman, Walt. LEAVES OF GRASS: INCLUSIVE EDITION. Ed. Emory Holloway. Garden City,
    NY: Doubleday & Company, Inc., 1926.

ABOUT THE AUTHOR

Kurt Slauson was born in Sacramento, CA USA in 1970; his family moved from Albuquerque, NM to Ithaca, NY in 1976 where he grew up, with a summer in Madrid, Spain and a year in Bern, Switzerland, traveled widely in Europe; graduated from the University of Oregon, lived a bookstore year in Tennessee, earned his MA in English from the University of Montana, pursued PhD studies (abd) at the University of Victoria in British Columbia, Canada, taught English; received an AA in Culinary Arts at the Art Institute of Seattle, worked several years in the food industry; ten years in horticulture followed; he currently lives in Kelowna, BC.

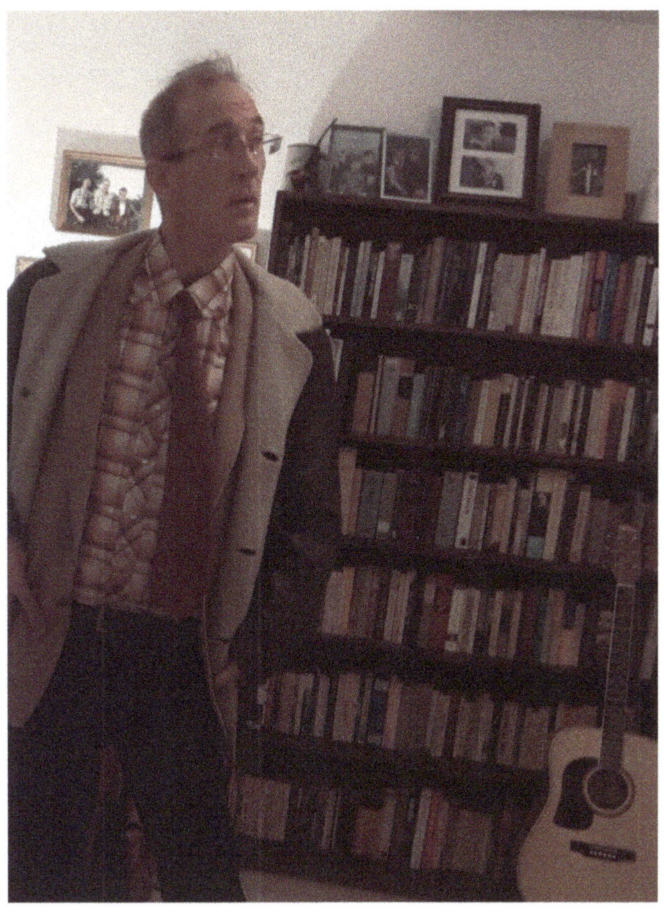

www.ingramcontent.com/pod-product-compliance
Lightning Source LLC
Chambersburg PA
CBHW042045030726
47599CB00019B/2372